Violence and Development along the India-Pakistan Border in Jammu & Kashmir

Deep Pal · Surya Valliappan Krishna · Saheb Singh Chadha

Violence and Development along the India-Pakistan Border in Jammu & Kashmir

Impact of Ceasefire Violations on SDGs 3, 4, and 8

Deep Pal
Ashoka University
Rajiv Gandhi Education City,
Haryana, India

Surya Valliappan Krishna
Carnegie India
Shaheed Jeet Singh Marg,
Delhi, India

Saheb Singh Chadha
Carnegie India
Shaheed Jeet Singh Marg,
Delhi, India

ISBN 978-3-031-84926-8   ISBN 978-3-031-84927-5   (eBook)
https://doi.org/10.1007/978-3-031-84927-5

© The Editor(s) (if applicable) and The Author(s), under exclusive license to Springer Nature Switzerland AG 2025

This work is subject to copyright. All rights are solely and exclusively licensed by the Publisher, whether the whole or part of the material is concerned, specifically the rights of translation, reprinting, reuse of illustrations, recitation, broadcasting, reproduction on microfilms or in any other physical way, and transmission or information storage and retrieval, electronic adaptation, computer software, or by similar or dissimilar methodology now known or hereafter developed.
The use of general descriptive names, registered names, trademarks, service marks, etc. in this publication does not imply, even in the absence of a specific statement, that such names are exempt from the relevant protective laws and regulations and therefore free for general use.
The publisher, the authors and the editors are safe to assume that the advice and information in this book are believed to be true and accurate at the date of publication. Neither the publisher nor the authors or the editors give a warranty, expressed or implied, with respect to the material contained herein or for any errors or omissions that may have been made. The publisher remains neutral with regard to jurisdictional claims in published maps and institutional affiliations.

Cover illustration: © Melisa Hasan

This Palgrave Macmillan imprint is published by the registered company Springer Nature Switzerland AG
The registered company address is: Gewerbestrasse 11, 6330 Cham, Switzerland

If disposing of this product, please recycle the paper.

Acknowledgements This work was supported by the British Academy under Grant Sustainable Development Program SDP2/100222. The authors would also like to thank King's College London, Carnegie India, and Ashoka University for their support. In particular, Rudra Chaudhuri as principal investigator was fundamental in steering this project. The authors would also like to thank all the individuals who worked on this project at various points in time—Shibani Mehta, Raghuveer Nidumolu, Meha Shah, Shreyas Shende, Devika Makkat, Neetha Nair, Jyotsna Badrinarayan, Ifrah Butt, Dhruv Taware, and Anshuman Yadav. The authors graciously acknowledge the several anonymous stakeholders who provided their inputs for this project. The authors are grateful to Srinath Raghavan and Christopher Clary for their feedback and reviews. The authors would like to thank all other stakeholders not mentioned by name who contributed to this project.

Lastly, the authors recognise the support of their partners, friends, and families in supporting the authors during their work on this book.

Competing Interests The authors confirm that there are no relevant financial or non-financial competing interests to report.

Ethics Approval Details of Ethics Approval:
Name of Committee: Faculty of Social Science & Public Policy
Institution: King's College London
Approval Number: Not Applicable
Information on Informed Consent from Human Participants: The authors interviewed several stakeholders for this project. All interviews with stakeholders were preceded by a permission taking process, which involved communicating to them the details of the research project and data collection, the interview process, how their inputs would be utilized in a publication, and an assurance of anonymity. Only thereafter, consent was obtained to interview them and utilize their inputs in a publication.

CONTENTS

1	**Introduction**	1
	References	4
2	**The Status of Public Goods in J&K**	7
	References	9
3	**What Determines How SDGs Are Delivered?**	11
	Violence and the Response to It	18
	Existing Infrastructure	18
	Access to Infrastructure	19
	Efforts by the State: The Administration and Security Agencies	19
	Efforts by Non-state Actors: NGOs and the Private Sector	20
	Miscellaneous Factors	21
	Response to Disruption in the Delivery of Public Goods	21
	References	22
4	**Methodology**	23
5	**How Violence Affects Health, Education, and Economic Activity**	25
	First-Order Impact of Violence	26
	Second-Order Impact of Violence	33
	The Impact of Violence on Infrastructure, Access, and Awareness	34
	Responses by the State	39

vii

viii CONTENTS

	Efforts by Non-state Actors	48
	References	50
6	**Conclusion**	63
	References	65

About the Authors

Deep Pal was a post-doctoral fellow at Ashoka University, India, and a researcher on the project "Living on the Line of Control: Mapping Lives, Violence, and Development." His research and publications focus on the Indo-Pacific, regional security of South Asia (with an emphasis on China), and peace studies. He holds a doctorate in international studies from the University of Washington.

Surya Valliappan Krishna is the associate director of projects and operations at Carnegie India. His responsibilities include development, communications, finance, and research project management. He manages partnerships with key stakeholders and executes development strategies as part of the operations team. He also oversees the communications team to help craft the organization's external strategy. Additionally, he assists the finance team with budget management, forecasting, and grant compliance. His research interests are India-Pakistan relations, border security, and cross-border violence. In particular, he works on the nature and dynamics of cross-border violence and its impact on civilian communities. Surya has a bachelor's degree in psychology from Christ University, Bengaluru, and an M.A. in terrorism, security, and society from the Department of War Studies, King's College London.

Saheb Singh Chadha is a senior research analyst in the Security Studies Program at Carnegie India. His research focuses on China's foreign and security policies, India-China relations, and India's military modernization. He is broadly interested in the geopolitics of South Asia and the Indo-Pacific. He is also a researcher on the project "Living on the Line of Control: Mapping Lives, Violence, and Development." Saheb's work has been published in the *Hindustan Times, Indian Express*, the *Print*, the *Diplomat, Firstpost, Financial Express*, and *Annapurna Express*. He has also appeared in the media and on podcasts such as *StratNewsGlobal, All Things Policy* and *India Today Global*. Saheb holds a bachelor's degree in political science with a minor in international relations and a diploma in advanced studies and research from Ashoka University, India.

Abbreviations

BADP	Border Area Development Programme
BSF	Border Security Force
CFV	Ceasefire violations
IB	International Border
INR	Indian National Rupee
J&K	Jammu & Kashmir
LoC	Line of Control
MHA	Ministry of Home Affairs
MHRD	Union Ministry of Human Resources Development
MNREGA	Mahatma Gandhi National Rural Employment Guarantee Act
NGO	Non-Governmental Organization
PHC	Primary Health Centre
PoK	Pakistan-occupied Kashmir
PTSD	Post-Traumatic Stress Disorder
ReT	Rehbar-e-Taleem
SDG	Sustainable Development Goals
SDH	Sub-District Hospital
SHC	Secondary Health Centre
SSA	Sarva Shiksha Abhiyan
UT	Union Territory

LIST OF FIGURES

Fig. 3.1	What determines the delivery of SDGs?	12
Fig. 3.2	Number of ceasefire violation incidents in J&K between 2002–21 [2]	14
Fig. 5.1	Average CFVs per day between 2014–2020 [2]	26
Fig. 5.2	Civilian fatalities and injuries due to CFVs between 2014–20 [5]	27
Fig. 5.3	Children aged five who attended pre-primary school during 2019–20, border districts under study [10]	28
Fig. 5.4	Literacy rate, border districts under study, 2011 [14]	29
Fig. 5.5	Jammu & Kashmir percentage distribution of net state domestic product by sector at current prices, 2020–21 [24]	30
Fig. 5.6	Cultivators and agricultural laborers as a percentage of total working force, border districts under study, 2011 [27]	31
Fig. 5.7	Employment generated through Rural Employment Generation Programme, border districts under study, 2003–20 [27]	32
Fig. 5.8	Cross-LoC trade, 2008–13 [33]	33
Fig. 5.9	District-wise healthcare infrastructure, border districts under study, as on 31 March 2022 [48]	35
Fig. 5.10	Average number of bank branches per 100,000 people, border districts under study, March 2020 [64]	39

Fig. 5.11 Households with any usual member covered under a health insurance/financing scheme, border districts under study, 2020 [84] 43

CHAPTER 1

Introduction

Abstract This chapter introduces the study. It delves into the importance of the issue, the relevance of the study, case study selection, and the key research questions. They are—how is everyday life affected by cross-border violence and the response to it in Jammu and Kashmir? What role do government agencies, the military, private sector, civil society, and local elites play in the delivery of public goods? And finally, what policy measures, taken both at the central and state levels, have been effective, and where do gaps still exist?

The chapter then lists the findings and key takeaways, reviews the work in this field, and lays down the structure of the manuscript.

Keywords Jammu · Kashmir · Ceasefire violation · Border · Line of Control · Sustainable Development Goals · SDGs · Government schemes · State capacity

On September 6, 2022, an incident of cross-border firing in the Arnia sector of Jammu and Kashmir (J&K) was widely reported for an unusual reason [1]. It was the first incident of a ceasefire violation (CFV) along the Line of Control (LoC) between India and Pakistan in nineteen months. The February 2021 reaffirmation of a 2003 ceasefire agreement by the

© The Author(s), under exclusive license to Springer Nature
Switzerland AG 2025
D. Pal et al., *Violence and Development Along the India-Pakistan Border in Jammu & Kashmir*,
https://doi.org/10.1007/978-3-031-84927-5_1

1

two countries led to a sharp reduction in CFV incidents in villages along the border, easing restrictions and normalizing life [2]. This has led to the acceleration of development projects, including improvements to physical and digital infrastructure.

Even in J&K, which has experienced intense periods of violence over the last three decades, parts of border districts closest to the LoC and the International Border (IB) stand out due to the impact of the violence emanating from the relations between the armed forces of India and Pakistan on daily life. Kathua, Samba, and Jammu districts lie along the IB, while the districts of Poonch, Rajouri, Baramulla, and Kupwara lie along the LoC. As per the 2011 census, the total population in these border districts is 5,462,934, which accounts for 43.55 percent of the population of the erstwhile state of Jammu and Kashmir [3]. A significant part of this population resides in villages along the LoC and the IB.

This study asks: How is everyday life affected by cross-border violence and the response to it in Jammu and Kashmir? What role do government agencies, the military, private sector, civil society, and local elites play in the delivery of public goods? And finally, what policy measures, taken both at the central and state levels, have been effective, and where do gaps still exist? This study aims to address these questions by examining the effect of cross-border violence on the daily lives of residents in border villages as reflected in three crucial sustainable development goals (SDGs) formulated by the United Nations. These are good health and wellbeing, quality education, and decent work and economic growth—SDGs 3,4, and 8, respectively.

It finds that disruptions in daily life can be categorized into confinement, displacement, and migration. The violence (defined here as CFVs and the response to them) prevents access to educational institutions, hospitals, and places of employment; it thwarts the operation of businesses and the training and employment of professionals while restricting access to services such as roadways and telecommunication facilities. Between 2014 and 2020, 13,160 incidents of violence were recorded along the LoC and the IB that separates the union territory (UT) of J&K from Pakistan. These incidents killed 125 civilians and injured 675 others [4]. Avoiding casualties requires regular evacuation of villagers from affected areas and housing them in temporary camps, army barracks, and other buildings till CFVs cease. In 2018, for instance, 160,000 people were displaced due to shelling incidents [5]. Similarly, in August and October 2014, over 32,000 people living along the IB and the LoC were forced to leave their homes and take shelter in camps set up by the government [6]. To be clear, CFVs are one amongst several other factors such as geographical and socio-political trends that are responsible for the lack of development in the border areas. However, this study focuses on drawing out the nuances of how exactly CFVs and the resultant responses from the state stunt development in the border areas, as this phenomenon is understudied.

The study also finds that the unique conditions of the region have engendered a governance approach that prioritizes security, in turn leading to a greater military governance mandate rather than a civilian one in border areas. This has resulted in an atrophying of the civilian administrative machinery and lower state capacity. Schemes like the Border Area Development Programme (BADP), the central government's flagship program for development projects run by the Ministry of Home Affairs (MHA) in border regions across the country, have initiated projects related to infrastructure, education, and health in J&K [7]. However, these face implementation barriers due to several challenges, including improper assessment of the needs of the communities, absence of adequate awareness of the program amongst intended beneficiaries, lack of coordination between the center and the states, funding, lack of convergence amongst various development schemes, absence of local bodies for implementing the program, and geographical and climatic constraints [8]. [Stakeholder C5, virtual interview, August 2022.]

Similarly, Sadbhavana (translated as "goodwill"), the primary military-civic action program under which the Indian Army delivers public goods in border areas, has attempted to plug some of the gaps in the delivery of health, education, and economic opportunities [9]. As the name suggests, it flows from an approach aimed at generating goodwill amongst civilians, particularly those in the border areas as part of its "hearts and minds" approach [10]. [Stakeholder A4, virtual interview, June 2021; Stakeholder D3, virtual interview, July 2021.]

While the program offers facilities where almost none exist, initiatives under Sadbhavana are often ad-hoc and inconsistent. [Stakeholder D5, virtual interview, June 2021; Stakeholder F7, virtual interview, July 2021.] They depend on the availability of funds and the discretion of the local commanding officer. [Stakeholder E2, virtual interview, February 2021; Stakeholder D3, virtual interview, July 2021.]

While data about all of J&K is available in some detail from government and private sources, there is a substantial gap in research conducted specifically with border areas in mind. The relationship between violence and the status of public goods in J&K has been explored briefly in the context of the health sector, with little attention to the impact on education and economic activities. There is a dearth of detailed, district-level data on the present status of the public goods, whether it is health, education, or economic activity, which makes it difficult to understand the context in, and the extent to, which health, education, and economic opportunities are impacted by violence. Moreover, while some attempts have been made to understand the impact of flagship government initiatives such as the Sarva Shiksha Abhiyan, no studies have considered the role and efficacy of all stakeholders—government and non-government—as a whole [11].

The following sections examine the current status of SDG delivery in J&K, with a special focus on border areas. Thereafter, the study develops and defines an analytical framework for the impact of violence on delivery of good health and wellbeing, quality education, and economic opportunities in border communities. This framework is operationalized in the section that follows along with an analysis of the role that the government, the armed forces, and non-governmental actors play.

References

1. 2022. Pakistan Violates Ceasefire along International Border in Jammu. Economic Times, September 6. https://economictimes.indiatimes.com/news/defence/pakistan-violates-ceasefire-along-international-border-in-jammu/articleshow/94021168.cms.
2. Joint Statement. 2021. Press Information Bureau, Government of India. https://pib.gov.in/PressReleasePage.aspx?PRID=1700682. Accessed 5 January 2023.
3. Jammu and Kashmir Religion, Caste Data—Census. 2011. Jammu and Kashmir Population Census, Census India. https://www.censusindia.co.in/states/jammu-kashmir. Accessed 13 January 2023.
4. Ceasefire Violations by Pakistan. 2017. Press Information Bureau, Government of India. https://pib.gov.in/newsite/PrintRelease.aspx?relid=168802. Accessed 13 December 2022; Unstarred Question No: 2981. 2018. Parliament of India, Lok Sabha, Government of India. https://loksabha.nic.in/Questions/QResult15.aspx?qref=64622&lsno=16. Accessed 13 December 2022; Unstarred Question No: 149. 2021. Parliament of India, Lok Sabha, Government of India. https://loksabha.nic.in/Questions/QResult15.aspx?qref=18780&lsno=17. Accessed December 13, 2022.

5. India: Figure Analysis—Displacement Related to Conflict and Violence. 2019. Internal Displacement Monitoring Centre, ACAPS. https://www.acaps.org/sites/acaps/files/key-documents/files/grid_2019_-_conflict_fig ure_analysis_-_india.pdf. Accessed 13 December 2022.

6. 2014. J&K: 2014 Records 562 Ceasefire Violations; Highest in 11 Years. Economic Times, December 28. https://economictimes.indiatimes.com/news/politics-and-nation/jk-2014-records-562-ceasefire-violations-highest-in-11-years/articleshow/45667451.cms; 2014. Kashmir: Civilians Flee as Border Clashes Continue. BBC News, October 8 https://www.bbc.com/news/world-asia-india-29532066.

7. About the Border Area Development Programme. Border Area Development Programme, Ministry of Home Affairs, Government of India. https://badp.mha.gov.in/. Accessed January 12, 2023.

8. Manoharan, N., Depak Saravanan, Vasvi Saini, and Srijana Karnatak. 2019. Secure Through Development: Evaluation of India's Border Area Development Programme. *Strategic Analysis* 44:1–14. https://doi.org/10.1080/09700161.2020.169999.

9. Anant, Arpita. 2011. Counterinsurgency and "Op Sadhbhavana" in Jammu and Kashmir. Manohar Parrikar Institute for Defence Studies and Analyses, last modified n.d. https://idsa.in/occasionalpapers/Counterinsurgen cyandOpSadhbhavanainJammuandKashmir. Accessed 20 June 2023.

10. Question No. 897. Parliament of India, Rajya Sabha, Council of States, Government of India. https://pqars.nic.in/annex/208/Au897.pdf. Accessed 9 January 2023.

11. Kaul, Shashi and Shradha Sahni. 2012. Assessment of Sarva Shiksha Abhiyan in Jammu City. *International Journal of Educational Sciences* 4:57–66. https://doi.org/10.1080/09751122.2012.11890028.

CHAPTER 2

The Status of Public Goods in J&K

Abstract The chapter begins by situating the study in the broader literature, arguing that there is a lack of research on the effects of ceasefire violations on border populations in Jammu & Kashmir. It then focuses on the status of public goods (healthcare, education, and economic opportunity) in the areas under study. It details the challenges unique to J&K, particularly to the border areas of J&K.

Keywords Jammu · Kashmir · Sustainable Development Goals · SDGs · Health · Education · Employment · Economic activity

Much of the scholarship on J&K is focused on investigating the genesis of the conflict, understanding the state and non-state actors, and situating the violence on a broader regional and international canvas [1]. There has been some recent attention on CFVs, but purely to understand how they impact conflict escalation dynamics between India and Pakistan and to offer policy recommendations to reduce such incidents and manage India-Pakistan tensions [2]. What has been significantly absent in the literature is a methodologically rigorous study on the effect of CFVs on border populations, driven by data gathered from these communities.

© The Author(s), under exclusive license to Springer Nature
Switzerland AG 2025
D. Pal et al., *Violence and Development Along the India-Pakistan Border in Jammu & Kashmir*,
https://doi.org/10.1007/978-3-031-84927-5_2

NITI Aayog's data from 2020–21 offers some insights on how J&K fares on health, education, and economic opportunity in comparison to other parts of India. On parameters of health, J&K performs relatively better than education and economic activity. Overall, the UT scores 70/100 for SDG 3 (health), 49/100 for SDG 4 (education), and 47/100 for SDG 8 (economic wellbeing). In comparison, other remote and difficult-to-access states are in a relatively better position—for instance, Mizoram scores 79/100 for SDG 3, 60/100 for SDG 4, and 51/100 for SDG 8. Other small border states like Meghalaya (70/100 for SDG 3), Sikkim (58/100 for SDG 4), and Arunachal Pradesh (50/100 for SDG 8) score similarly, if not better, on the indicators [3].

This would suggest that challenges that emerge from insufficient staffing in health facilities, poor enrolment in schools, and rising unemployment are not unique to J&K. However, even among comparable populations, J&K seems worse off. For example, according to NITI Aayog data, J&K had only sixteen medical practitioners for every 10,000 people in 2020–21. On the other hand, the neighboring state of Himachal Pradesh with similar terrain and population density has sixty-six medical practitioners for every 10,000 people [4]. Finally, if J&K is a frontrunner on SDG 3 and does poorly on SDGs 4 and 8, Himachal Pradesh, which has challenges of access similar to J&K, does better on all three fronts—it scores 78/100 for SDG 3, 74/100 for SDG 4, and 78/100 for SDG 8.

Unlike in Himachal Pradesh, the challenges for J&K are significantly exacerbated by a history of conflict in general and cross-border violence in the border areas in particular. Challenges specific to fragile border communities include, for instance, a higher number of cases of mental illness. Studies have indicated that indefinite curfews, detentions, cordon and search operations, and identification checkpoints generate "collective experiences of alienation, vulnerability, and powerlessness" [5]. However, data collected on health and wellbeing often does not consider the impact of mental health issues except considering data on death by suicide [6]. The delivery of health, education, and economic opportunities across J&K has been particularly affected since 2019—first due to security measures after Article 370 was revoked in August 2019 and then the COVID-19 lockdown in 2020–21 [7]. "Complete communications blockades," referring to a shutdown of telephone and internet, along with restrictions on movement, have hindered the delivery of public goods [8].

REFERENCES

1. See Krepon, Michael, Rodney W. Jones, and Ziad Haider. Eds. 2004. *Escalation Control and the Nuclear Option in South Asia.* Washington, D.C.: Henry L. Stimson Center; Yusuf, Moeed. 2018. *Brokering Peace in Nuclear Environments: U.S. Crisis Management in South Asia.* Stanford: Stanford University Press; Ganguly, Sumit. 2016. *Deadly Impasse: Indo-Pakistani Relations at the Dawn of a New Century.* Cambridge: Cambridge University Press; Reidel, Bruce. 2013. *Avoiding Armageddon: America, India, and Pakistan to the Brink and Back.* Washington, D.C.: Brookings Institution Press; Perkovich, George and Toby Dalton. 2016. *Not War Not Peace: Motivating Pakistan to Prevent Cross-Border Terrorism.* New York: Oxford University Press; Cohen, Stephen P. 2013. *Shooting for a Century: The India-Pakistan Conundrum.* Washington, D.C.: Brookings Institution Press; Wolpert, Stanley. 2010. *India and Pakistan: Continued Conflict or Cooperation?* Oakland: University of California Press; Sagan, Scott D. Ed. 2009. *Inside Nuclear South Asia.* Stanford: Stanford University Press; Ganguly, Sumit and S. Paul Kapur. 2010. *India, Pakistan, and the Bomb: Debating Nuclear Stability in South Asia.* New York: Columbia University Press; Jalal, Ayesha. 2008. *Partisans of Allah: Jihad in South Asia.* Cambridge: Harvard University Press; Musharraf, Pervez. 2006. *In the Line of Fire: A Memoir.* New York: Free Press; Hussain, Zahid. 2008. *Frontline Pakistan: The Struggle with Militant Islam.* New York: Columbia University Press; Sidhu, Waheguru Pal Singh, Bushra Asif, and Cyrus Samii. Eds 2006. *Kashmir: New Voices, New Approaches.* Boulder, CO: Lynne Rienner; Paul, T. V. Paul. Ed. 2005. *The India-Pakistan Conflict: An Enduring Rivalry.* Cambridge: Cambridge University Press; Kux, Dennis. 2006. *India-Pakistan Negotiations: Is Past Still Prologue?* Washington, D.C.: United States Institute of Peace Press; Tellis, Ashley J., C. Christine Fair, and Jamison Jo Medby. 2001. *Limited Conflicts Under the Nuclear Umbrella: Indian and Pakistani Lessons from the Kargil Crisis.* Santa Monica: RAND Corporation.
2. Jacob, Happymon. 2019. *Line on Fire: Ceasefire Violations and India-Pakistan Escalation Dynamics.* New Delhi: Oxford University Press.
3. SDG India Index & Dashboard 2020–21: Partnerships in the Decade of Action. 2021. NITI Aayog. https://sdgindiaindex.niti.gov.in/assets/Files/SDG3.0_Final_04.03.2021_Web_Spreads.pdf. Accessed 13 December 2022.
4. Table 8: State-wise Density of Population. 2022. Reserve Bank of India. Last modified November 24, 2021. https://m.rbi.org.in/scripts/Publications View.aspx?id=20667. Accessed 13 December 2022; "SDG India Index."
5. Hoffman, Bruce and Haley Duschinski. 2014. Contestations Over Law, Power and Representation in Kashmir Valley. *Interventions* 16:501–30. https://doi.org/10.1080/1369801X.2013.816077.

6. NITI Aayog Uses the Sub-indicator of Suicide Rate (Calculated per 100,000 Population) to Incorporate an Understanding of Wellbeing. This Rate is 2.1 for Jammu and Kashmir.
7. Connah, Leoni. 2021. Double Lockdown in Kashmir during the Covid-19 Pandemic. *Peace Review* 33:33–38. https://doi.org/10.1080/10402659.2021.1956128.
8. Ibid.

CHAPTER 3

What Determines How SDGs Are Delivered?

Abstract This chapter explores the various axes along which the study has been carried out—i.e. the factors affecting the delivery of public goods related to SDGs 3, 4, and 8. These are—the first and second-order effects of violence, the response of the state to violence, existing infrastructure in the region under study, access to this infrastructure, policy efforts by state and non-state actors, miscellaneous factors such as politics & gender, and lastly, the responses of border communities to disruption in the delivery of public goods.

Keywords Jammu · Kashmir · Cross-border violence · Infrastructure · Health · Education · Employment · Indian Army · SDGs · Sustainable Development Goals · Ceasefire violations

The direct impact of CFVs on daily life in the form of loss of life, injuries, and the inability to carry out normal activities is easily visible. However, the indirect effects of violence continue during periods of relative quiet in between incidents of shelling. Cross-border violence has ebbed and flowed over the last two decades. Violence touched record levels preceding a November 2003 ceasefire between India and Pakistan. While 2004–07 was relatively peaceful, 2008 marked the beginning of a

© The Author(s), under exclusive license to Springer Nature Switzerland AG 2025
D. Pal et al., *Violence and Development Along the India-Pakistan Border in Jammu & Kashmir*,
https://doi.org/10.1007/978-3-031-84927-5_3

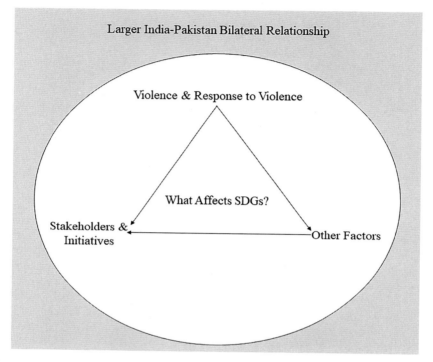

Fig. 3.1 What determines the delivery of SDGs?

spike in CFVs. The upward trajectory of cross-border incidents started again in 2013 and continued till 2020. The strength of the bilateral relationship between India and Pakistan has an impact on the escalation or de-escalation of cross-border violence. When relations between the two countries improve, the level of violence remains low; similarly, when the bilateral relationship suffers, escalation is seen along the border, which, in turn, affects daily life and the delivery of key SDGs [1] (Fig. 3.1).

The second-order effects of violence involve the impact of the response to it on the lives of locals, and violence over long periods amplifies geographical and sociopolitical difficulties. Actions by state and non-state actors from across the border trigger both administrative and military reactions. These responses reflect in curfews, shutdowns, communication blockades, an increased presence of the military, and a decreased presence of state administration. Over time, not just violence, but the overall permeance of the security apparatus as a part of the state's response to tackling forms of violence impacts daily life. For instance, in some cases, residents in villages close to the LoC are required to carry identity cards that need to be verified by security forces before they are allowed to travel in or out of the villages. Similarly, residents are dependent on security forces to lift curfew restrictions to be able to access schools, health centers, and places of employment after a CFV.

Beyond these are factors related to inhospitable terrain and weather, difficulties in conducting administrative and political tasks, and social and political unrest, many of which are common to border regions elsewhere in India. However, as is explained through comparisons between J&K and these regions throughout this book, in the area under study, cross-border violence and the response to it interact with these factors to affect the delivery of SDGs. While medical professionals and teachers are often disinclined to take up remote postings, the threat of violence adds an extra layer of disruption to the delivery of these services in J&K. For instance, while the total number of physicians, nurses, and midwives per 10,000 population stand at sixteen across J&K, for Mizoram and Meghalaya, the numbers are fifty and twenty-five, respectively.

CFVs are defined in this study as actions undertaken by a state or non-state actor or a combination of the two to inflict violence or react to provocation near or across the LoC and the IB between India and Pakistan. CFVs on the Indian side are the result of three kinds of situations: escalation by Pakistan's armed forces targeting military posts and civilian areas, militant activity on and across the border, and infiltration from Pakistan-occupied Kashmir (PoK) by militants, often with cover fire from Pakistan's security personnel, into India. Apart from the death of civilians, these lead to grievous injuries, confinement, displacement, restricted access to services, and damage to essential infrastructure (Fig. 3.2).

By border areas, this project refers to parts of the seven border districts that lie along the IB and the LoC. While all of J&K suffers from less-than-ideal delivery of public goods, villages along the border between India and Pakistan persistently undergo more difficulties when it comes to opportunities for inclusive education, appropriate healthcare, and adequate employment. While urban centers and areas away from the

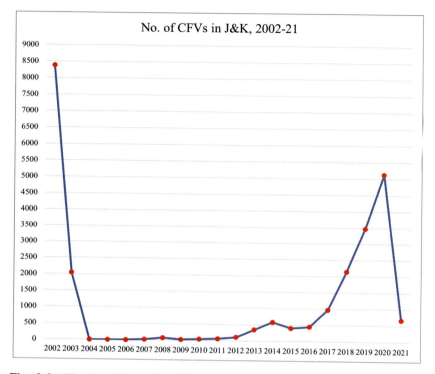

Fig. 3.2 Number of ceasefire violation incidents in J&K between 2002–21 [2]

border also experience violence, the nature of and underlying factors for such incidents are significantly different.

The following framework is organized to understand the ways in which violence affects the lives of border communities as well as the cascading effect of violence on the available facilities and opportunities of daily life. As an added layer, it examines how geographical and sociopolitical conditions interact with violence to affect the delivery of health, education, and economic opportunities (Table 3.1).

3 WHAT DETERMINES HOW SDGS ARE DELIVERED? 15

Table 3.1 The delivery of SDGs

Indicators	SDG 3: Good health and wellbeing	SDG 4: Quality education	SDG 8: Decent work and economic growth
Effects of CFVs and the response to violence	– How does it impact health? – How does it impact healthcare infrastructure? – How does it impact access to healthcare? – How does it impact efforts by various actors?	– How does it impact student learning? – How does it impact education infrastructure? – How does it impact access to education? – How does it impact efforts by various actors?	– How does it impact various sectors of economic activity? – How does it impact mobility and access to work? – How does it impact job opportunities? – How does it impact efforts by various actors?
Existing infrastructure	– What is the equipment and staffing situation in health facilities? – Is electricity supply and telecommunication consistent and sufficient?	– What is the equipment, syllabus, and staffing situation in schools? – Is electricity supply and telecommunication consistent and sufficient?	– What is the state of financial infrastructure? – What are the employment opportunities in public organizations and in the private organized and unorganized sectors? – Is electricity supply and telecommunication consistent and sufficient?

(continued)

16 D. PAL ET AL.

Table 3.1 (continued)

Indicators	SDG 3: Good health and wellbeing	SDG 4: Quality education	SDG 8: Decent work and economic growth
Access to infrastructure	– How near and affordable are health facilities? – What communication and transport services are available to people? – How do climate and terrain impact access? – What is the demographic makeup of those looking for health facilities in border areas?	– How near and accessible are schools? – What communication and transport services are available to people? – How do climate and terrain impact access? – What is the demographic makeup of those looking for educational opportunities in border areas?	– How near and accessible are banks, ATMs, and other financial services? – What communication and transport services are available to people? – How do climate and terrain impact access? – What is the demographic makeup of those looking for economic opportunities in border areas?
State efforts	– What policy measures exist? – Are policies being implemented? – How coordinated are policies? – How are they trying to reduce the impact of cross-border violence? – What impact does violence have on policy implementation?	– What policy measures exist? – Are policies being implemented? – How coordinated are policies? – How are they trying to reduce the impact of cross-border violence? – What impact does violence have on policy implementation?	– What policy measures exist? – Are policies being implemented? – How coordinated are policies? – How are they trying to reduce the impact of cross-border violence? – What impact does violence have on policy implementation?

(continued)

3 WHAT DETERMINES HOW SDGS ARE DELIVERED? 17

Table 3.1 (continued)

Indicators	SDG 3: Good health and wellbeing	SDG 4: Quality education	SDG 8: Decent work and economic growth
Non-state efforts	– What programs, one-time measures, and advocacy are private actors and NGOs carrying out? – How easy/hard is it for NGOs to operate?	– What programs, one-time measures, & advocacy are private actors and NGOs carrying out? – How easy/hard is it for NGOs to operate?	– What programs, one-time measures, & advocacy are private actors and NGOs carrying out? – How easy/hard is it for NGOs to operate?
Miscellaneous factors	– Is there enough awareness about health facilities? – How does politics affect healthcare? – How does social unrest affect healthcare? – How does gender impact health outcomes? – What is the impact of migration in and out of the border areas?	– Is there enough awareness about educational opportunities? – How does politics affect education? – How does social unrest affect education? – How does gender impact education outcomes? – What is the impact of migration in and out of the border areas?	– Is there enough awareness about economic opportunities? – How does politics affect economic activity? – How does social unrest affect economic activity? – How does gender impact economic activity? – What is the impact of migration in and out of the border areas?

(continued)

18 D. PAL ET AL.

Table 3.1 (continued)

Indicators	SDG 3: Good health and wellbeing	SDG 4: Quality education	SDG 8: Decent work and economic growth
Response to disruption in SDG delivery	– How do people cope with the lack of health facilities? – What alternative arrangements do they seek? – How does the lack of facilities due to violence affect the decision to migrate, temporarily or permanently?	– How do people cope with the lack of educational opportunities? – What alternative arrangements do they seek? – How does the lack of opportunities due to violence affect the decision to migrate, temporarily or permanently?	– How do people cope with the lack of economic opportunities? – What alternative arrangements do they seek? – How does the lack of opportunities due to violence affect the decision to migrate, temporarily or permanently?

VIOLENCE AND THE RESPONSE TO IT

The obvious and most important consideration for the framework are the ways in which CFVs directly impact health, education, and economic activity. When such incidents occur, civilian communities are confined to their homes and are unable to undertake regular activities, including accessing schools, hospitals, and places of employment. They often leave their places of residence to either individual and community bunkers or areas away from their villages for weeks or months. This displacement has medium- to long-term impact and affects entire communities, thereby multiplying the impact on the region.

Apart from the impact on humans, the violence and the response to it extract a cost through damage to infrastructure, including roads, schools, health centers, and places of work. It also involves the loss of domesticated animals and damage to farmland. Additionally, it impacts efforts by state and non-state actors to build and maintain facilities and implement policies for the delivery of public goods. The fear of impending violence also acts as a barrier to accessing facilities, staffing schools and medical facilities, and setting up industries in border areas. The response to violence from state actors slows down private and civil society organizations working in these areas as they must go through several layers of scrutiny and verification.

Existing Infrastructure

A region's infrastructure is the fundamental vehicle for service delivery and achieving development goals. Schools are critical for education, hospitals for health, and banks for financial services. Studying existing infrastructure in border areas offers an understanding of facilities available to people there. For all SDGs, infrastructure is evaluated based on the equipment and human resources present in government and private facilities as well as associated facilities that help run them. For health and education, this refers to the presence of physical infrastructure, and for economic opportunities, to the availability of options for employment. Evaluating the state of physical connectivity, such as roads, airways, alternative routes, and available transportation, as well as digital connectivity is also necessary. The state of infrastructures like power and telecommunication is a factor that affects all three SDGs under the focus of this study.

Access to Infrastructure

A survey of infrastructure needs to also consider the means to access these facilities to determine whether people in border areas can access the services available to them. For example, for ease of access (especially during an emergency), primary healthcare centers must be within reasonable physical proximity. The same goes for schools and Anganwadi centers so that regular attendance is not hindered. The access to infrastructure must be evaluated along two parameters—physical proximity and affordability. This study examined the role of geographical elements such as terrain and climate in impacting access to facilities during periods of disruption due to violence. For instance, the lack of roads or inclement weather in remote parts of Kupwara and Poonch adds to the complications of accessing healthcare facilities when cross-border violence breaks out. Elsewhere, internet and mobile connectivity suffer due to signal jammers operated by the Indian Army, interrupting economic activity. While factors such as terrain and weather are independently significant in determining access to health, education, and economic opportunities, this study restricts itself to considering their impact only when they add to the effect of cross-border violence in affecting life.

EFFORTS BY THE STATE: THE ADMINISTRATION AND SECURITY AGENCIES

Efforts by various state actors at the central and local levels to deliver the SDGs under review were also evaluated. The government impacts SDGs through the allocation of budgets and planning for service delivery, actual service delivery and development, providing infrastructure and the access to it, and enabling other stakeholders to effectively play their part. For example, in 2017, the MHA constituted a "study group" to examine the problems faced by people residing near the IB and the LoC in the wake of regular ceasefire violations [3]. The absence of government can also affect SDGs since it is the principal stakeholder responsible for the delivery of education and health services and for providing economic opportunities. These efforts are represented in policy responses such as a scheme for Mobile Medical Units under the National Health Mission or in the evacuation of civilians during cross-border firing [4].

For J&K, the security forces, including the Indian Army and paramilitary personnel such as the Border Security Force (BSF), form a large part of the mechanism for delivering public goods. Along with providing security, they help in the delivery of health and education services and enable economic opportunities. Sometimes, the presence of these forces inhibits the effective functioning of daily life, such as when agricultural fields are used to build security infrastructure or as minefields. This scenario is also characterized by restrictions on movement, heavy security personnel deployment, military infrastructure being prioritized over civilian infrastructure, atrophying of civilian administration, and the expansion of the role played by security personnel.

EFFORTS BY NON-STATE ACTORS: NGOS AND THE PRIVATE SECTOR

While non-state stakeholders rarely have the scale or the expertise to make up for the lack of government infrastructure, NGOs as well as the private sector are critical in their attempts to identify gaps left by other stakeholders. NGOs engage in data collection, advocacy, and awareness campaigns and initiate long-term programs or standalone measures—as in the demand for a comprehensive compensation policy for victims of cross-border violence [5]. Similarly, they have also researched and raised awareness around mental health in J&K [6]. However, their functioning is hindered by the absence of physical and human resources along with periodic outbreaks of violence. Moreover, scrutiny from the security agencies also restricts NGO activity in regions closer to the border. [Stakeholder D2, virtual interview, June 2021; Stakeholder J2, virtual interview, August 2022.] As a result, villages close to the IB and the LoC have intermittent NGO activity—a fact that is usually issue-based rather than region-specific.

The private sector affects the deployment of SDGs by way of infrastructure and investment, albeit in a limited way. This could be in the form of private healthcare centers and schools, small and medium cottage industries that employ local communities, or investment in skill development or local agro-based industries. The private sector's interest is guided largely by factors such as ease of doing business, the possibility of running a successful enterprise without interruption or loss of business days, and the availability of human resources.

Miscellaneous Factors

Certain miscellaneous variables cut across SDGs (and state and non-state efforts) in their impact on the lives of border communities and are included in this study. The success of public or private efforts depends a great deal on whether the intended beneficiaries are aware of the schemes meant for them. Similarly, sociopolitical factors such as political instability, elections, protests and civilian unrest, and shutdowns—even when disconnected from cross-border violence—affect the delivery of public goods. The regional politics played an important role, especially since the members of the legislative assembly were often the first point of contact for civilian needs. However, bringing the region under the jurisdiction of the central government in 2019 has interrupted the collective bargaining abilities of communities. District development councils have recently been set up to give a voice to these communities and act as intermediaries between the villagers and the officers of the state. Another crucial factor is gender, as the fallout of the violence disproportionately impacts women's health, education, and employment opportunities.

Finally, repeated periods of CFVs and the subsequent disruptions eventually break down local communities, leading people to migrate, sometimes permanently. Such events leave a permanent impact on the social and economic fabric of the region.

RESPONSE TO DISRUPTION IN THE DELIVERY OF PUBLIC GOODS

It is important to understand how locals deal with the absence of public goods and the ramifications of the strategies they adopt. Alternative mechanisms replace traditional service providers—for instance, faith healers come to the fore when trained medical professionals are unavailable, and informal *mohalla* schools—which refer to a teacher residing in a village organizing informal classes for students in the vicinity—gain prominence when traditional education is interrupted. It is to be noted that differences in impact exist even within the border communities—the challenges of service delivery, food security, and capital and infrastructure access are more acute for nomadic communities like Gujjars and Bakarwals.

REFERENCES

1. Krishna, Surya Valliappan. 2022. Bordering on Peace: Evaluating the Impact of the India-Pakistan Ceasefire. Carnegie India. https://carnegieindia.org/2022/02/24/bordering-on-peace-evaluating-impact-of-india-pakistan-ceasefire-pub-86513. Accessed 11 January 2023.
2. For data for 2002–03, see 2018. Pakistan Violated Ceasefire 633 Times in Two Months: Govt. Indian Express, April 4. https://indianexpress.com/article/india/pak-violated-ceasefire-633-times-in-2-months-govt-5123152/; for data for 2004–06, see Cease Fire Agreement (CFA) Violations by Pakistan in Jammu and Kashmir: 2004–2020. South Asia Terrorism Portal, Institute for Conflict Management. https://www.satp.org/datasheet-terrorist-attack/india-jammukashmir/JK-CFA-2004-2020. Accessed 25 April 2022; for data for 2007–13, 2017, and 2021, see Majid, Zulfikar. 2021. Ceasefire Violations by Pakistan along J&K Border Declined Sharply in 2021. Deccan Herald, December 24. https://www.deccanherald.com/national/north-and-central/ceasefire-violations-by-pakistan-along-jk-border-declined-sharply-in-2021-1064192.html; for data for 2014, see 2014. J&K: 2014 Records 562 Ceasefire Violations; Highest in 11 Years. Economic Times, December 28. https://economictimes.indiatimes.com/news/politics-and-nation/jk-2014-records-562-ceasefire-violations-highest-in-11-years/articleshow/45667451.cms?from=mdr; for data for 2015–16, see Unstarred Question No: 679. 2017.

Parliament of India, Lok Sabha, Government of India. https://loksabha.nic. in/Questions/QResult15.aspx?qref=58617&lsno=16. Accessed 11 January 2023; for data for 2018–20, see Ceasefire Violations and Terrorist Attacks. 2021. Press Information Bureau, Government of India. https://pib.gov.in/ PressReleasePage.aspx?PRID=1694506. Accessed 11 January 2023.

3. Unstarred Question No: 5973. 2018. Parliament of India, Lok Sabha, Government of India. https://loksabha.nic.in/Questions/QResult15.aspx? qref=67841&lsno=16. Accessed 11 January 2023.

4. Mobile Medical Units (MMUs). National Health Mission, Ministry of Health and Family Welfare, Government of India. https://nhm.gov.in/index1.php? lang=1&level=2&sublinkid=1221&lid=188. Accessed 11 January 2023.

5. Unstarred Question No: 3708. 2014. Parliament of India, Lok Sabha, Government of India. https://loksabha.nic.in/Questions/QResult15.aspx? qref=10557&lsno=16. Accessed 11 January 2023; 2016. Guv Urged to Rehabilitate Persons Rendered Disabled in Shelling. Daily Excelsior, February 14. https://epaper.dailyexcelsior.com/2016/02/14/?id=45053.

6. Muntazar Kashmir Mental Health Survey Report 2015. 2015. Médecins Sans Frontières (MSF), University of Kashmir, and Institute of Mental Health and Neurosciences. https://www.msfindia.in/sites/default/files/ 2016-10/kashmir_mental_health_survey_report_2015_for_web.pdf. Accessed 11 January 2023.

CHAPTER 4

Methodology

Abstract This chapter elaborates on the methodology and sources utilised by the study. These are—insights from national and local newspapers between 2004–2020, data collected from civil society organizations, relevant journal articles and reports, government data at the local and national level, and extensive parsing of peer-reviewed journals across multiple disciplines for relevant pieces on health, education, and economic activity in J&K. Significantly, it was also informed by around sixty in-depth stakeholders interviews conducted between 2020 and 2022, with serving and retired government officials, members of the armed forces, members of civil society, academics, journalists, and others. Finally, field visits to the region assisted in primary research and data collection to substantiate findings from secondary sources. They helped understand local realities ensuring all sides to the complex issues were adequately reflected in the outcome.

Keywords Ceasefire violations · India-Pakistan · Jammu · Kashmir

The study uses a variety of sources, including primary data, to arrive at a coherent narrative of the effect of CFVs on everyday life. To understand the nature and dynamics of cross-border violence, it relies on data

© The Author(s), under exclusive license to Springer Nature
Switzerland AG 2025
D. Pal et al., *Violence and Development Along the India-Pakistan Border in Jammu & Kashmir*,
https://doi.org/10.1007/978-3-031-84927-5_4

from the India-Pakistan Ceasefire Incidents Project, a rigorously developed dataset and dashboard on CFVs from both sides of the LoC and the IB. Led by Rudra Chaudhuri, the project represents trends in kinetic activity from 2004.

As often is the case with research on Jammu and Kashmir, the study faced a scarcity of consistent district-level data collected by either government or non-government stakeholders. This is compounded by the exceptional remoteness of border areas and the fact that they do not feature as administrative entities for data collection in official studies. The COVID-19 pandemic has added to these complications. The study attempts to overcome this by rigorous triangulation and plotting broad trend lines. The insights in the study are sourced through a comprehensive review of open-source data and literature on daily life in J&K with a specific focus on border districts.

This includes insights from national and local newspapers between 2004 and 2020, data collected from civil society organizations focused on health, education, or economic opportunities in the region, and select relevant scholarship. Data collected by local and central government ministries and departments, annual reports, state and national surveys, white papers, memos, and legislative and parliamentary records, including questions and debates in the Lok Sabha and the Rajya Sabha spanning almost two decades, contribute to the study.

In addition, an expansive literature review of 1078 peer-reviewed journals across multiple disciplines was conducted for relevant pieces on health, education, and economic activity in J&K. It has been informed by around sixty in-depth stakeholder interviews conducted between 2020 and 2022. The stakeholders include serving and retired government officials, members of the armed forces, members of civil society, academics, journalists, and others. These stakeholders are anonymized and represented in the book through an alphanumeric code, eg. Stakeholder E1, Stakeholder B2. Finally, the study is supported by field visits to the region to better understand local realities and multiple perspectives on the topic.

CHAPTER 5

How Violence Affects Health, Education, and Economic Activity

Abstract This chapter forms the essence of the book and undertakes a deep dive into the study, the argument, the findings, and the takeaways. It explores the role played by the effects of violence, infrastructure, state & non-state actors, and miscellaneous factors, on the public goods under Sustainable Development Goals 3, 4, and 8.

Keywords Jammu · Kashmir · Line of Control · Cross-border violence · Development · Public goods · Infrastructure · Border villages · Education · Literacy rates · Agrarian economy · Mental health

Former J&K chief minister Omar Abdullah alluded to the impact of cross-border violence on economic life when he said that tension at the LoC and the IB in J&K directly impacts development activities [1]. This includes the availability of economic opportunities as well as challenges in running education and health facilities. Settlements close to army pickets undergo maximum damage as military posts are among the first targets in CFVs, resulting in collateral damage to the civilian infrastructure around them, including schools and health centers. [Stakeholder E1, virtual interview, February 2021.] Fatality or injury to earning members of the family, damage to property and livestock, halting of agricultural, business, and

© The Author(s), under exclusive license to Springer Nature
Switzerland AG 2025
D. Pal et al., *Violence and Development Along the India-Pakistan Border in Jammu & Kashmir*,
https://doi.org/10.1007/978-3-031-84927-5_5

27

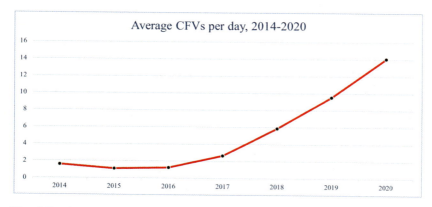

Fig. 5.1 Average CFVs per day between 2014–2020 [2]

tourism activity, and delay in development initiatives and infrastructure development add to the economic cost (Fig. 5.1).

First-Order Impact of Violence

The most obvious effects of CFVs are death and maiming caused by firing, shelling, and mortar fire from across the border. Sometimes, shells do not explode on impact and are triggered when unsuspecting civilians chance upon them, leading to injuries or death [3]. [Stakeholder F7, virtual interview, July 2021.] The army undertakes drives specifically to destroy unexploded shells [4]. Mines laid almost three decades ago to deter infiltration carried out under the cover of CFVs shift position during rains, landslides, earthquakes, and avalanches. [Stakeholder D3, virtual interview, July 2021.] As a result, they sometimes injure civilians unaware of their presence. [Stakeholder C2, virtual interview, July 2021.] (Fig. 5.2).

Continued violence over the years and slow development of remedial infrastructure have resulted in little focus on the education sector in vast stretches of villages along the border in J&K. NITI Aayog data for 2020–21 put the union territory at the bottom of the ladder in both enrolment ratio in elementary education as well as proficiency in students in middle school [6]. According to 2017 figures from the J&K education department, over 32,500 schools in the state lacked basic facilities such as toilets, drinking water, buildings, and libraries [7]. NITI Aayog data

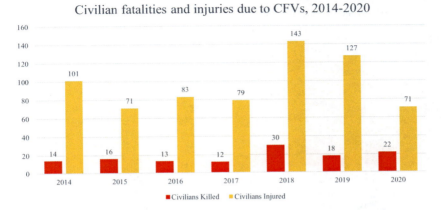

Fig. 5.2 Civilian fatalities and injuries due to CFVs between 2014–20 [5]

from 2020–21 suggests that around 80 percent of schools in J&K have some of these basic facilities. In comparison, 83 percent of the schools in similarly remote Mizoram, and 99 percent of schools in Sikkim, have these basic infrastructures [8].

The disruption reflects in the results of students in public examinations. In 2020, the government promised action after a poor showing by government schools in the tenth standard examinations, including a few schools in Bandipora, Baramulla, and Kupwara, where student pass percentage was below 20 percent and, at times, zero [9] (Fig. 5.3).

Due to low population density and inadequate infrastructure, some students in border communities travel as far as 20 kilometers to reach school [11]. This becomes impossible when violence breaks out. At the same time, an end to violence does not necessarily mean a return to normalcy. In many cases, anxious villagers prefer to not send their children to school for weeks even after restrictions are lifted. [Stakeholder E4, virtual interview, February 2021.] This problem is particularly acute in the case of female students, who are often kept at home citing safety issues, in the absence of reliable public transport services and the possibility of violence erupting at short notice. [Stakeholder F8, virtual interview, August 2021; Stakeholder D3, virtual interview, July 2021.]

The government has flagged this problem, highlighting the increase in the dropout rate across the region from 6.93 percent and 5.36 percent

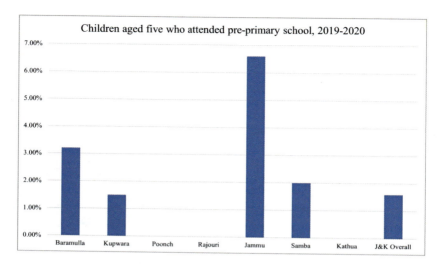

Fig. 5.3 Children aged five who attended pre-primary school during 2019–20, border districts under study [10]

in primary and upper-primary schools respectively in 2015–16 to 10.30 percent and 10.20 percent respectively in 2016–17 [12]. In 2020–21, the rate amongst primary school students was as high as 3.9 percent for J&K, while in border states with similar terrain, such as Sikkim, there were almost no dropouts [13]. Other states with similar issues of access demonstrate a far higher literacy rate. For 2021, with 76 percent, J&K was at the lower end of small border states as far as literacy for children aged fifteen years and above was concerned. The figure was 98 percent for Mizoram, 94 percent for Nagaland, and 91 percent for Meghalaya [8] (Fig. 5.4).

While cross-border violence seldom targets educational institutions deliberately, they are inevitably damaged in the shelling [15]. [Stakeholder D7, virtual interview, March 2021.] In July 2017, for instance, over 260 students and teachers were trapped in their school in Nowshera in Rajouri as cross-border hostilities broke out. They were eventually rescued, but the school building was damaged by mortar fire [16]. The next year, students in a school in the same district were stranded once again when cross-border firing started, managing to leave only after the firing stopped [17]. Depending on the seriousness of the conflagration, schools stay shut

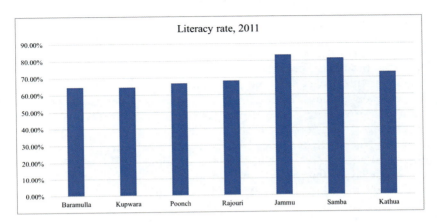

Fig. 5.4 Literacy rate, border districts under study, 2011 [14]

for periods extending from a few days to a few weeks. In July 2016, shelling along the LoC in Poonch and Rajouri forced schools to stay shut for two consecutive weeks [18]. In a separate incident in 2018, the J&K government decided to temporarily shut over 500 schools along the LoC, affecting over 6,000 students [19].

The instability brought about by violence reduces avenues available for economic activity. By all measures, the unemployment rate in J&K has continued to be worse than the national average for a sustained period [20]. While NGOs, the government, the army, and other stakeholders undertake some skill development for the youth, unemployment is a real crisis in the region. [Stakeholder F2, virtual interview, February 2021.] While tourism offers a key avenue for employment, it is the first to get hit when violence strikes. An increase in cross-border violence slows tourist arrival and affects seasonal and permanent employment in hotels, restaurants, transportation, and handicrafts sectors [21]. Conversely, the peace that has prevailed after February 2021 has allowed tourism to prosper in the border areas such as Gurez in Bandipora and Teetwal in Kupwara [22].

The problem is compounded by the lack of stability and the constant threat of violence, discouraging fresh private investment into the region. Investors are disincentivized by remoteness, poor connectivity, high transport costs, frequency of power outages, poor infrastructure, weak resource base, sparse population density, and, critically, the fact that periodic violence or the possibility of violence makes it difficult to address these issues [23]. The lack of private investment has drastically reduced opportunities for job creation (Fig. 5.5).

Almost three-fourths of the population of J&K depends directly or indirectly on agriculture [25]. However, while the contribution of agriculture to gross state domestic product has reduced in recent years, the dependence of the population on the sector has not [26] (Fig. 5.6).

It also means that though the economy in the region is agrarian, growth in agriculture and allied services continues to be stagnant [28]. In border areas, this stagnation coincides with the loss of agricultural workdays either directly because of cross-border violence or indirectly because of displacement due to evacuations. Additionally, farmlands along the border are often used by the security forces for operational purposes such as building bunkers, watchtowers, or approach roads, which render the land uncultivable [29]. [Stakeholder F4, virtual interview, July 2021; Stakeholder D3, virtual interview, July 2021.] The question of delays in and even lack of compensation due to crop loss and use of land for official purposes have been raised repeatedly [30]. [Stakeholder D3,

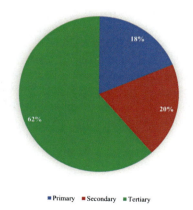

Fig. 5.5 Jammu & Kashmir percentage distribution of net state domestic product by sector at current prices, 2020–21 [24]

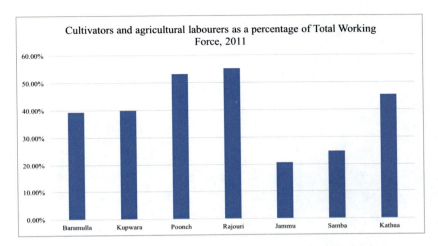

Fig. 5.6 Cultivators and agricultural laborers as a percentage of total working force, border districts under study, 2011 [27]

virtual interview, July 2021; Stakeholder C5, virtual interview, August 2022.] However, no comprehensive standardized policy on compensation mechanisms for livestock and damage to property has been formulated.

Cross-border shelling also limits the movement of those working as laborers. [Stakeholder F7, virtual interview, July 2021.] While the Mahatma Gandhi National Rural Employment Guarantee Act (MNREGA) is an important employer for daily-wage earners, firing and shelling incidents prevent individuals from traveling to access economic opportunities under the scheme, sometimes for long periods. [Stakeholder D11, virtual interview, August 2021.] (Fig. 5.7).

During heavy shelling incidents, villages and communities are evacuated to bunkers or safer areas away from the border. Such incidents of violence lead to the army or other agencies restricting access to certain areas for civilians. This affects Pahadi or Gujjar communities who are engaged in woodwork, grazing sheep, or collecting medicinal plants, all of which becomes impossible to undertake. [Stakeholder F4, virtual interview, July 2021.] At other times, villages lie between the fence along the LoC and the delineated border or zero line, leading to restricted movement. [Stakeholder F4, virtual interview, July 2021; Stakeholder F5, virtual interview, March 2021.]

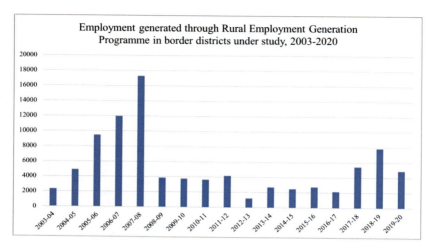

Fig. 5.7 Employment generated through Rural Employment Generation Programme, border districts under study, 2003–20 [27]

Cross-LoC trade has been an important part of Kashmir's economy. By some accounts, the trade, based on a barter system of twenty-one permitted items, amounted to INR 75 billion and created 1,70,000 job days between 2008 and 2019 [31]. The freight revenue from this trade is believed to have earned transporters around INR 650 million and employed truck drivers, laborers, restaurant owners, gas station employees, and automotive repairmen [32]. The exchange was carried out through trade facilitation centers set up in Salamabad in Uri with Muzaffarabad across the LoC and in Chakan-da-Bagh in Poonch with Rawalakot across the LoC. However, political and security considerations have often trumped the economic logic of the exchange, leading to it being discontinued in 2019 (Fig. 5.8).

During the decade-long trade, inadequate infrastructure and financial facilities along the border prevented the scaling up of the facilities [34]. The disruption to cross-LoC trade often coincided with the escalation of violence between the two sides [35]. This had economic consequences—in 2013, for example, losses to traders and farmers due to such interruptions were estimated at INR 16 million, with no policy of compensation from the government [36]. As of 2021, over 25,000 people only in Uri and Poonch were believed to be directly affected by

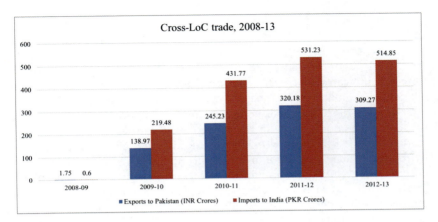

Fig. 5.8 Cross-LoC trade, 2008–13 [33]

interruptions to bilateral trade, while around ten times that number were indirectly affected. [Stakeholder B1, interview, June 2022; Stakeholder F11, virtual interview, August 2022.]

SECOND-ORDER IMPACT OF VIOLENCE

CFVs have also left imprints beyond those that are immediately visible. These second-order effects include a deep psychological impact. Residents of villages close to the LoC have reported being unable to sleep during CFV incidents [37]. Some have called this a feeling of "living in the conflict situation" [38]. Their experience is emblematic of the experience of border communities. The threat of unpredictable violence creates constant fear and uncertainty, causing mental health issues such as post-traumatic stress disorder (PTSD), stunted psychological development, depression, and anxiety [39]. [Stakeholder F9, virtual interview, June 2021; Stakeholder F10, virtual interview, April 2021.] Children are particularly vulnerable as they do not understand what a CFV is or why it happens [40]. [Stakeholder F7, virtual interview, July 2021; Stakeholder F10, virtual interview, April 2021.] CFVs are accompanied by prolonged curfews, detentions, and cordon and search operations. Residents have reported experiencing "alienation, vulnerability, and powerlessness" because of these measures [41].

A 2015 study found greater incidences of PTSD, depression, and anxiety in border districts. Baramulla and Kupwara, along the border, reported 51 and 58 percent prevalence of mental health issues, respectively, as compared to 28–38 percent in non-border districts [42]. Research indicates that even substance dependence and abuse may be connected to long-term exposure to conflict. [Stakeholder F10, virtual interview, April 2021.] Sixty-four percent of respondents in a study on substance dependence in the region reported witnessing multiple traumatic events [43]. Those working with deaddiction efforts in the region worry about increasing alcohol addiction. Additionally, the availability of heroin, along with cannabis and medicinal opioids, has been a problem. [Stakeholder F9, virtual interview, June 2021; Stakeholder C2, virtual interview, July 2021.] People usually begin with oral consumption, subsequently transitioning to injectables. [Stakeholder C2, virtual interview, July 2021; Stakeholder C4, virtual interview, August 2022.]

The Impact of Violence on Infrastructure, Access, and Awareness

By the J&K government's admission, healthcare infrastructure in border areas is inadequate for the mental and physical health challenges in the region [44]. Primary Health Centres (PHCs) can rarely operate in the remote and dangerous terrain close to the LoC and up to 10 kilometers away from it. [Stakeholder D3, virtual interview, July 2021; Stakeholder C5, virtual interview, August 2022.] Sub-district hospitals (SDHs) like the one in Uri suffer from the lack of basic infrastructure such as consistent electricity supply' [45]. The district hospital in Bandipora only operationalized its blood bank in late 2021 despite several years of demands by the local population' [46] Adverse terrain, cross-border violence, and infrastructure raised to respond to the violence contribute to the poor state of healthcare. The border districts along the LoC, which include Poonch, Kupwara, Rajouri, and Baramulla, are mountainous whereas the border districts along the IB, including Samba, Kathua, and Jammu, are more accessible. Expansion in health infrastructure has been uneven due to these constraints [47]. Kupwara and Srinagar are emblematic of this problem. While Srinagar has dedicated infrastructure for chest diseases, kidney ailments, and ophthalmology departments, Kupwara has no such facilities. [Stakeholder D4, virtual interview, June 2021.] There is also a severe lack of mental health wards or psychosocial intervention. [Stakeholder C2, virtual interview, July 2021.] Similarly, in Poonch, any case requiring special healthcare is usually referred to the hospitals in Srinagar or Jammu, the two divisional headquarters. [Stakeholder D3, virtual interview, July 2021.] In some cases, healthcare centers remain unusable after being damaged by cross-border firing. [Stakeholder D7, virtual interview, March 2021.] (Fig. 5.9).

Given that the compensation is the same for border and non-border areas, healthcare professionals find no incentive to serve in a region with increased violence and threats to personal safety. [Stakeholder C2, virtual interview, July 2021; Stakeholder C5, virtual interview, August 2022.] As a result, even where healthcare facilities such as PHCs and Secondary Health Centres (SHCs) exist, they suffer from staffing shortages [49]. [Stakeholder C5, virtual interview, August 2022.] Doctors posted in border areas often do not take up their post, either using political connections to get the decision reversed or taking a leave of absence. [Stakeholder D3, virtual interview, July 2021; Stakeholder C2, virtual interview, July 2021.] In rare cases, a doctor attends the facility once or twice a week. The number of PHCs in districts like Poonch (forty-four in 2020–21) and Rajouri (fifty-five in 2020–21) is higher than in similarly

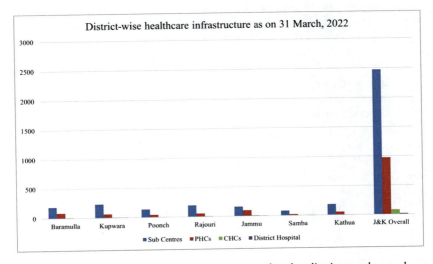

Fig. 5.9 District-wise healthcare infrastructure, border districts under study, as on 31 March 2022 [48]

remote districts elsewhere in India, such as West Khasi Hills in Meghalaya (sixteen in 2020–21) or Changlang in Arunachal Pradesh (seven in 2020–21) [50]. However, the lived experiences of the border communities in J&K suggest that despite the existence of facilities, staffing shortages lead to services being unavailable.

This staffing problem is considerably worse for mental health. All of J&K suffers from a dearth of adequate psychologists and psychiatrists. [Stakeholder F10, virtual interview, April 2021.] In Kashmir, those who do practice are largely concentrated in and around Srinagar. [Stakeholder C2, virtual interview, July 2021.] Thus, people living in the border areas do not have the means to address the mental health issues caused by the virtue of their location. According to stakeholders in Kupwara, there is just one psychiatrist for the entire district of around 900,000 people who is posted in the district headquarters, away from the border [51]. [Stakeholder C2, virtual interview, July 2021.] The lack of mental healthcare facilities, the stigma around mental health, and a religious society mean that faith healers are often the first recourse. [Stakeholder C2, virtual interview, July 2021.] The stigma surrounding mental health is considerably higher among women. [Stakeholder F9, virtual interview, June 2021.]

The process of employing teachers in border schools has had long-standing problems, marked by inadequate numbers, reluctance to work in remote and dangerous areas, and disgruntlement over pay and other facilities. Teachers, facing the same conditions as students, would often stay away from schools after sustained periods of cross-border shelling out of the fear of resumption of violence. The government's decision to punish them, as in the case of Rajouri in 2018, when twenty-five teachers were suspended for not being present in school, has only increased the reluctance of teachers to serve in these areas [52]. Teachers have claimed that their pay is not commensurate with the risks of a difficult posting, pointing out that they get a lower housing allowance in difficult areas and have to make their own arrangements to travel great distances to and from schools [53]. [Stakeholder J2, virtual interview, August 2022; Stakeholder C5, virtual interview, August 2022.]

Telecom and internet connectivity along the border is very poor and further limits access to health, education, and economic opportunities. [Stakeholder F4, virtual interview, July 2021.] Villages in remote border areas are seldom serviced by anything beyond 2G mobile data. [Stakeholder D5, virtual interview, June 2021.] Security concerns have delayed the improvement of mobile networks. Additionally, during incidents of violence, internet and communication blackouts, even preemptive ones, are common [54]. As a result, even though telemedicine facilities have been launched, slow internet speed makes them unviable [55]. In some cases, doctors using services such as WhatsApp to connect with poorly staffed SDHs reported having their networks disrupted. [Stakeholder F4, virtual interview, July 2021.]

Similarly, while online classes during the coronavirus pandemic may have helped students elsewhere to stay connected to their schools, it has acted as a barrier for students in the border villages of J&K. According to the Union Education Ministry, as of August 2021, 70 percent of students across J&K did not have access to any digital devices, suggesting that they were incapable of attending online classes [13]. While the data does not specify how many of them resided in border areas, considering that these communities are among the poorest in the region, it follows that a sizeable proportion of the border population is covered by this number. For those in the remaining 30 percent that reside in border areas, having access to a device is not enough. Students often travel long distances to be able to access an area where they can download online lessons and participate in class [56]. [Stakeholder J2, virtual interview, August 2022.] These factors have contributed to a higher incidence of students dropping out of school, more so among female students [57].

When it comes to healthcare, the landscape is complicated by cross-border violence that creates additional barriers to accessing healthcare. The violence and its threat deter movement, impeding the ability to travel to PHCs, SHCs, and SDHs. This is particularly acute in the case of pregnant women and is visible in the high maternal mortality rate in these areas. As of April 2022, the ratios for Poonch and Baramulla were 104 and seventy-four, respectively, while the same for Srinagar was zero [58]. In an area where CFVs and their aftermath routinely injure local people, the delay in accessing healthcare worsens the condition of the patient and even leads to death in some cases. [Stakeholder F7, virtual interview, July 2021; Stakeholder D6, virtual interview, July 2021.] When healthcare is not readily available, people are asked to visit private facilities or must be airlifted for better care in the cities [59].

Accessibility of healthcare facilities is also impaired by curfews aimed at monitoring and preventing violence. Villages are often cordoned off with restricted movement after sunset, which means that locals cannot access PHCs. [Stakeholder F7, virtual interview, July 2021.] Sometimes, entire villages near the border are fenced, resulting in limited access for locals. In places, the fencing is as far inland as a couple of kilometers from the LoC, constraining villagers between the fence and the border and restricting access to healthcare. [Stakeholder F4, virtual interview, July 2021.] To access non-border areas where civilian hospitals and schools are located, villagers need to have their identity cards checked by security forces. Understandably, the armed forces prioritize security responsibilities. Tasks such as facilitating movement and attending to medical contingencies come second [60]. The verification process can take hours of precious time during a medical emergency. [Stakeholder F7, virtual interview, July 2021; Stakeholder F4, virtual interview, July 2021; Stakeholder F8, virtual interview, August 2021.] Even if one were allowed to exit a border village, the many roadblocks and security checkpoints on the way to facilities outside the border area hinder and delay access to healthcare. [Stakeholder A4, virtual interview, June 2021.]

Continued incidents of violence often lead to the use of school buildings and other facilities as shelters for evacuated populations or security personnel, rendering them unavailable for their original purpose [61]. School buildings, often the only concrete structure around, offer the best available refuge for villagers fleeing sustained cross-border violence. At other times, the sheer number of evacuees requires that schools be used as temporary camps, during which all associated infrastructure, including facilities for serving mid-day meals, are used to house and feed the displaced villagers. The schools stay shut till the evacuees are sent back to their villages. [Stakeholder D2, virtual interview, June 2021.]

Violence and the threat of it also slow down the access to financial and non-financial infrastructure and capital as well as credit. Recent data from NITI Aayog has highlighted concerns about opportunities for economic growth across J&K. The region performs poorly on indices including ease of doing business. While the number of households covered under Prime Minister Jan Dhan Yojana is high, the number of functioning branches and ATMs is low per 100,000 population, indicating a problem of financial access that is more acute in remote areas along the border [6]. In 2013, for example, the central government rolled out its direct cash transfer scheme across the country. However, the scheme was not implemented in J&K in the first phase due to the non-availability of an adequate number of banks in rural areas and the absence of other requisite facilities' [62]. J&K has among the lowest number of banks per 100,000 people among smaller border states. For instance, in 2020–21, the number stood

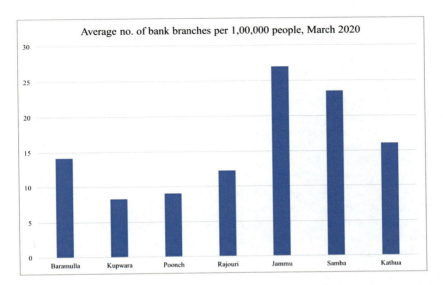

Fig. 5.10 Average number of bank branches per 100,000 people, border districts under study, March 2020 [64]

at fourteen per 100,000 people in comparison to eighteen for Mizoram and twenty-five for Sikkim [63] (Fig. 5.10).

The question of access is acute not just for villagers but also for the local administration officials in border areas who have a more limited mandate compared to the security agencies. Decades of security presence, constant violence, and the role of security forces in taking the lead in responding to this violence have rendered the local administration ineffective. [Stakeholder D2, virtual interview, June 2021.] A loss of access and physical absence in the region have made it difficult for the civilian administration to work toward the delivery of education, health, and economic opportunities in border communities. [Stakeholder D3, virtual interview, July 2021.]

Responses by the State

Along with local and central governments' efforts, the army plays a major role in providing adequate health and education facilities as well as economic opportunities in the border areas of J&K. A study group set up in 2017 to look at issues faced by border communities visited the border villages in the districts of Jammu, Samba, Kathua, Rajouri, and Poonch [65]. Based on its recommendations, steps including the building of bunkers and compensation for damage to crops, livestock, and so on by cross-border firing at par with the norms of the National Disaster Response Force have been initiated.

In 2006, five working groups were set up to examine J&K's development requirements [66]. They recommended policies on compensation to next of kin of victims of militancy, pension to widows of the civilians killed in militancy-related violence, scholarships to orphans affected by militancy, return rehabilitation packages for Kashmiri migrants, strengthening of people-to-people contacts across the LoC, and the promotion of cross-LoC trade. They also emphasized the need to bring greater efficiency in governance along with transparency and accountability into the systems and processes in J&K [67].

The security situation, particularly in rural and remote areas, often does not permit normal administrative and commercial activities to take place. In J&K, the BADP projects related to infrastructure, education, and health have been implemented with the assistance of local administrations as part of a comprehensive approach to border management [68]. These projects relate to social infrastructure, link roads, employment generation, agriculture, and allied sectors amongst other aspects like education and healthcare. Additionally, the projects under the army-run Sadbhavana initiative to address gaps in education, health, employment, and youth and women empowerment are managed at the local army commander level and are often not adequate alternatives to regular development work. Currently, the initiative has little coordination with local or central government initiatives.

The recent lull in cross-border violence due to the reaffirmation of the ceasefire between India and Pakistan in February 2021 has contributed to wellbeing in the area under study. For civilians in the area, this is a temporary relief from the high cost paid for living close to a conflict area. It has allowed the speeding up of long-pending developmental projects and led to policy changes such as the lifting of restrictions on expansion of telecommunication facilities. For those living along the LoC, this means better access to healthcare, educational resources, and economic opportunities. [Stakeholder J1, virtual interview, August 2022.] However, the overall lack of development persists despite a lull in violence.

The construction of bunkers for civilians to take refuge during CFVs is the most significant policy measure taken by the government to safeguard border residents. In 2018, the MHA approved the construction of 14,460 bunkers in the border districts of Samba, Jammu, Kathua, Poonch, and Rajouri [69]. This includes 1431 "community bunkers" and 13,029 "individual bunkers." As of December 2021, 8,500 of these are ready [70]. About 15,000 more bunkers are planned in subsequent phases [71]. However, the construction has sometimes been found to be faulty and subpar with issues like seepage. Tendering processes and cost escalations have been questioned, sometimes leading to the suspension of construction [72]. [Stakeholder C5, virtual interview, August 2022.] There have also been concerns that the bunkers may only be able to withstand low-caliber shelling [73]. Moreover, they are not optimal for people who are unable to move promptly, including pregnant women, old people, and children, or those tending to livestock, who are often reluctant to leave domesticated animals during incidents of violence. [Stakeholder F7, virtual interview, July 2021; Stakeholder D6, virtual interview, July 2021.]

The J&K government set up "cluster colonies" to reduce the impact of CFVs on border communities [74]. The colonies were meant to house entire affected populations at night while allowing them to travel to their villages during the day. In Kerni and Birhuti situated on the LoC, colonies were created 4–6 kilometers away from the original homes and fields. However, barring Kerni, the cluster colonies have not been operational since the summer of 2009 [75]. A more common strategy of temporarily evacuating border villagers to safer locations to prevent the loss of life is currently prevalent. In such cases, the district administration arranges medical care, shelter, and other services, including transportation to safer locations' [76]. For example, over 600 people living along the border in Jammu were shifted to safer locations following intense shelling by Pakistan in October 2013. They were housed in community centers with facilities that were out of the line of fire of the shelling [77].

As of 2019, the BADP has funded nine separate medical projects, including the construction of sub-centers that are the first points of contact in the primary healthcare system. These were allotted INR 110 million and are to be constructed in villages that are 1–10 kilometers away from the IB or the LoC, in Jammu, Samba, Kathua, and other border districts [78]. It has funded schemes such as "Aapka School Aapke Gaon" (translated as "your school, in your village") aimed at facilitating additional classes for students in villages within 5 kilometers of the LoC or the IB [79].

There have been concerns that infrastructure under the BADP is being concentrated in border areas that do not see CFVs rather than in areas that do. [Stakeholder D3, virtual interview, July 2021.] This is because violence makes it difficult to execute projects in the border areas; additionally, the absence of road infrastructure makes it difficult and expensive to transport construction materials and machinery. Moreover, the program is designed to address development requirements in several border states with varying social, economic, and political conditions, and there is little scope for customization for J&K. The BADP funding for J&K has stayed unchanged for years. It currently averages INR 40 crores per year, marginally higher than INR 35 crores in 2001–02 [80]. In fact, the current spending is far lower than in 2002–03, when INR 100 crores was released to J&K under the scheme [81]. The BADP is not exclusively aimed at improving the state of education or health access—its focus is also a wide range of development projects ranging from road-building to ensuring water supply [82].

Coinciding with the pause in CFVs in recent years, central government schemes have been launched to improve access to healthcare. In July 2022, the central government announced that under the SEHAT scheme of the Ayushman Bharat Pradhan Mantri Jan Arogya Yojna, 500,000 women associated with the J&K Rural Livelihood Mission would be provided with a health insurance cover of INR 500,000 for each individual's family [83]. [Stakeholder D8, interview, June 2022.] Locally called the "Golden Card," this allows them to avail services in government and private hospitals. Under the Gaon Ayushman initiative, the State Health Agency has also started reaching the "last villages, which remain cut from the rest of the world due to adverse weather conditions" [83]. [Stakeholder D8, interview, June 2022.]

While some of these efforts have been useful, major gaps in the availability and accessibility of health facilities persist. In his visit to border villages in Kupwara in October 2020, the J&K lieutenant governor acknowledged these access issues and allowed the use of his administration's helicopters in case of emergencies [84]. [Stakeholder D5, virtual interview, June 2021; Stakeholder C5, virtual interview, August 2022] (Fig. 5.11).

Efforts to improve health infrastructure have been made by the local government as well. In August 2021, the Directorate of Health Services

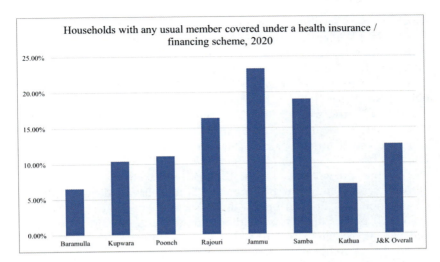

Fig. 5.11 Households with any usual member covered under a health insurance/financing scheme, border districts under study, 2020 [84]

in J&K began mobile health clinics for Rajouri, Poonch, Bandipora, Pulwama, Kupwara, and other border districts at the cost of INR 50 million [86]. Since 2021, medical officers in J&K's health and family welfare services who have been appointed based on being a resident of a Backward Area adjoining the LoC or the IB are required to serve in such border areas for at least seven years [87]. This has been viewed as the first step toward addressing the staffing gap. [Stakeholder C2, virtual interview, July 2021.] Similarly, medical students can now be posted to border areas for extra credit. [Stakeholder F9, virtual interview, June 2021.]

There has been less focus on mental health infrastructure because of multiple reasons including a lack of awareness and a greater focus on physical safety and compensation to people affected by cross-border violence. [Stakeholder F10, virtual interview, April 2021; Stakeholder C2, virtual interview, July 2021.] The district mental health program, which aims to train medical professionals in mental healthcare practices and increase awareness about mental health, has performed sub-optimally in the region [88]. This is due to the lack of clarity about the division of responsibilities between the J&K Department of Health and Medical Education, which oversees primary healthcare, and the J&K Directorate of Health Services, which oversees secondary healthcare. [Stakeholder F9, virtual interview, June 2021.] While the mental health program is present in some districts such as Pulwama, it is does not exist in others. [Stakeholder C2, virtual interview, July 2021.] According to locals, the development in Pulwama is attributed to the officer in charge of the district rather than an overall policy push. [Stakeholder C2, virtual interview, July 2021.] Due to insufficient psychiatric social workers or clinical psychologists, professionals with a master's degree but no experience in clinical settings and evaluation are posted in rural areas. [Stakeholder C2, virtual interview, July 2021.]

The impact of violence on education has been acknowledged as an issue by both central and state governments. Studies have indicated the need for additional facilities in border areas, such as one conducted in 2010 per which border districts of Kathua, Poonch, and Rajouri were identified as educationally backward and requiring extra attention [89]. At the state level, elected representatives have pushed the government to elicit promises of remedial classes for students in border schools [90]. However, the experience of border communities has seldom come up separately in policy discussions.

The J&K government has stepped in to bolster infrastructure and facilities. In 2016, an IT-enabled school management system was launched in partnership with agencies including the Union Ministry of Human Resources Development (MHRD) and the Indian Space Research Organisation to keep track of staff strength, student–teacher ratio, and other data about schools across the state [91]. Around the same time, specific policies to encourage more female students were undertaken, which included girls-only institutions and free books [92]. The government has also announced the construction of hostels for girls in remote areas, including Kupwara, Pulwama, and Rajouri [93].

In the late 1990s, the state government introduced the Rehbar-e-Taleem (ReT) scheme to resolve the issue of finding teachers willing to teach in border villages. The program, operated through the Sarva Shiksha Abhiyan (SSA) scheme, hired local people on contract to teach in primary schools in hard-to-reach areas, promising to eventually absorb them in regular government service. The aim was to staff schools in remote areas while tackling unemployment. The strategy was also lucrative for the government as hiring under the ReT was less expensive than hiring regular government employees.

The program was met with great enthusiasm, only to be mired in controversies and allegations [94]. [Stakeholder D3, virtual interview, July 2021; Stakeholder D4, virtual interview, June 2021.] Teachers have alleged that the government has delayed salaries and refused to absorb them [95]. ReT teachers have repeatedly resorted to strikes, affecting the efficacy of the program. By 2012, over 30,000 teachers were hired under the scheme, though only a handful of them were regularized [96]. [Stakeholder J2, virtual interview, August 2022.] ReT was eventually shut down in 2018. Teachers and staff who approached district authorities, claiming nonpayment of salaries, were told that the government had not released funds for their wages [97]. The issues with ReT indicate deeper structural inefficiencies within the system. Education audits held by district authorities have found students unable to answer questions from their syllabus or solve math problems, whereas in other cases, teachers have been found to not be conversant with their subjects [98]. In 2013, the state government suspended officials of the education department after they were found to be involved in the embezzlement of INR 70 lakhs [99]. Elected representatives have promised remedies but put the onus on teachers, claiming that it is them who must ensure that students do not suffer [100].

In 2016, the state's school education department categorized physical threats to schools in the state as normal, sensitive, and hypersensitive, with education department staff being deputed to ensure the protection of school infrastructure. However, responding to a question in the Rajya Sabha the same year, the MHRD said that it had received no proposal from the J&K government for assistance with closed or burnt schools in Kashmir under the SSA or the Rashtriya Madhyamik Shiksha Abhiyan schemes [101]. The dual challenge of unemployment and irregular classes has led to a focus on vocational and technical training in the state. The central government has rolled out programs for young people from areas in J&K without adequate facilities, encouraging them to enroll in institutions outside the state.

The governments have also rolled out schemes to assist employment, increase entrepreneurship, and ensure empowerment. These include Himayat, a skill-empowerment and employment scheme for those aged 18–35 years; Udaan, a scheme that is aimed at providing employment by imparting training in organized retail, financial services, information technology, telecom, infrastructure, oil and gas, hospitality, manufacturing, paramedics, and life sciences sectors [102]; and Umeed, a scheme to empower women from poor and vulnerable rural households by organizing them in self-help groups at the village and block levels [103]. However, these are often not tailored with the unique conditions in border areas in mind. For instance, while some initiatives encourage training in corporate environments, it is difficult to do so in border areas without the youth having to move out of their communities.

Despite the obvious lack of development and paucity of opportunities in the communities adjoining the border, there have been few policies either from the local or the central government aimed at the specific issues faced by these communities. Employment and job opportunity schemes are usually aimed at all of J&K, thereby failing to consider the specific social, economic, and political situation in the border villages, ending up with little impact on lives along the border. Additionally, outside of the MNREGA scheme, there is a lack of awareness about government schemes and programs in border areas. For example, despite the importance of the BADP in the region, there is little awareness about the mandate and benefits of the initiative amongst border populations. [Stakeholder D3, virtual interview, July 2021.]

At times, development attempts lead to unintended consequences, as with the 330-megawatt Kishanganga Hydroelectric Power Project meant to improve the lives of local communities. However, the operationalization of the project necessitated the migration of residents of border villages in Gurez and Bandipora. The dam has affected 610 families in Gurez and 171 families in Kralpora. While the project was well-intentioned, it has led to protests from local communities against the authorities [104].

The other major stakeholder in the delivery of public goods in the region is the Indian Army, which has the advantage of being present in remote areas along with the availability of trained personnel. In the Gurez sector, for example, the army provides electricity through its generator network. [Stakeholder D2, virtual interview, June 2021.] Elsewhere, it has helped by supplying solar lights in remote villages inhabited by the nomadic Gujjar and Bakarwal communities [105]. In times of high electricity demand, such as the winter months, the armed forces are often called upon to help by providing electricity.

The army is also a major employer in border regions. Locals are usually employed as porters on a need basis for INR 12,000–15,000 per month to help with the movement of goods for the army. [Stakeholder D3, virtual interview, July 2021.] The job carries the risk of injuries or even death [106]. Moreover, the recruitment system is informal, with no fixed rules for the process that must be followed. Additionally, employment is for limited durations and depends on the need and the discretion of the security forces. Many in the border communities also work as suppliers of various consumable goods to the security forces in the region. [Stakeholder D2, virtual interview, June 2021.] Despite the obvious drawbacks, these opportunities are highly sought after because of assured pay and are considered closest to a government job. [Stakeholder D5, virtual interview, June 2021.] In addition, regiments such as Jammu and Kashmir Light Infantry recruit primarily from border areas such as Poonch and Kupwara. [Stakeholder D6, virtual interview, July 2021.]

The army's efforts at providing public goods are mostly routed through the overarching Sadbhavana initiative. It has conducted free health camps, such as the one in Akhnoor in March 2016 and the Sadbhavana Mela in August 2016 within 2 kilometers of the LoC [107]. The camps include facilities for medical checkups and treatment, minor surgeries, blood tests, vaccinations, drug deaddiction lectures, and even veterinary checkups [108]. Medicines, clothes, ration packets, and essential items are also distributed in these camps [109]. In some cases, army doctors train locals in injury management and basic medical care [110]. Beyond Sadbhavana, security agencies provide healthcare near their camps whenever possible. In Kupwara, where the army has a substantial presence, facilities at the bases are open to local people. [Stakeholder D6, virtual interview, July 2021.] Villagers working as porters for the army, along with their families, also have access to healthcare. [Stakeholder D6, virtual interview, July 2021.] The army built COVID care centers in border areas such as Baramulla and Uri, even though the lack of coordination with the local administration has rendered them underutilized [111]. [Stakeholder D3, virtual interview, July 2021; Stakeholder D6, virtual interview, July 2021.]

The army has been offering education and training opportunities under the Sadbhavana initiative. Since the late 1990s, it has been running a program that allows students from border villages to travel outside J&K to visit places and institutions of interest across India. [Stakeholder E4, virtual interview, February 2021.] The visits are aimed at instituting interest about other parts of India as well as evoking ambition to avail of opportunities available outside J&K. [Stakeholder E2, virtual interview, February 2021.] According to the army, 7800 students participated in 264 such tours between 2014 and 2017 [112]. Sadbhavana offers skill development and educational opportunities and especially targets women and youth empowerment [113]. The program runs forty-six Goodwill Schools across J&K benefitting approximately 14,000 students who are provided scholarships and other support [114]. The army organizes career guidance talks, technical training camps, and skills awareness sessions in coordination with government agencies and financial institutions [115]. Some of these are directed specifically toward female students, where they are taught basic computer skills such as navigating the internet, data entry, and word processing [116]. The army also provides infrastructure, from furniture to computers, to existing educational facilities.

Even as border schools struggle with dilapidated structures, unscheduled closures, and irregular students, efforts under Sadbhavana have suffered due to uncoordinated and patchy policymaking. In places, local army units have helped fix buildings, only to realize that the school does not have other requisite facilities to hold classes. Elsewhere, computers arranged under government schemes or received as donations have arrived in schools without electricity connections [98].

Despite its efficacy, Sadbhavana is disconnected from the overall policymaking ecosystem, which explains some of the issues with coordination and aforementioned lapses. Additionally, the scheme is inherently ad-hoc as local army commanders are responsible for the execution of the program, resulting in changes in priorities as and when officers are transferred. [Stakeholder D1, virtual interview, March 2021.] Most importantly, the army is primarily guided by security-related objectives. As a result, Sadbhavana and other initiatives by the army are primarily guided by the objective of building relationships with the villagers. This separates Sadbhavana from other initiatives that have the delivery of public goods as their primary objective. In fact, it further complicates the position and the role of the civilian administration, which, in a landscape where security-related objectives are prioritized, is often sidelined and has to compete with the security forces for resources and access. [Stakeholder F4, virtual interview, July 2021; Stakeholder A2, virtual interview, July 2021.]

EFFORTS BY NON-STATE ACTORS

In much of the rest of J&K, NGOs fill gaps created by other stakeholders, particularly in the field of physical and mental health. In urban areas, away from the border, private players have started investing in economic development of the region and in building health and educational infrastructure. However, this is not the case in border areas. As a 2004 report explains, most NGOs are based around Srinagar, with very few in the border regions [117]. Private players, from civil society organizations to potential private healthcare providers face the same barriers in the border areas that other stakeholders do, including hostile terrain and violence as well as intense scrutiny and a lengthy verification process [118].

NGOs have been able to offer sporadic support, often with active assistance from administration. In 2016, for instance, the All J&K NGO Federation, along with the Samba district administration, organized a medical camp in villages 5 kilometers from the border [119]. Help Foundation, a local NGO, has worked with authorities for the rehabilitation of disabled children as well as children who have lost their limbs due to landmines. [Stakeholder F8, virtual interview, August 2021.] NGOs have also been involved in advocacy, as in the case of Viklang Chhatra Trust, which has been working to convince the government to provide financial support to the victims of cross-border violence and cover their medical expenses in Jammu, Samba, and other border districts [120].

In another instance, driven by the impact of the Kargil conflict on the border communities, Médecins Sans Frontières provided basic physical and mental healthcare in the border areas in a sustained manner in the 2000s. [Stakeholder F2, virtual interview, February 2021.] In 2013, the World Health Organization's Mental Health Gap Action Programme conducted a two-week training workshop for doctors and other medical practitioners from across J&K, including those from the border districts [121]. [Stakeholder F9, virtual interview, June 2021.] Acknowledging the gap in mental health services, civil society organizations have advocated for training a liaison psychiatry team for district hospitals, including those at the border. [Stakeholder F9, virtual interview, June 2021.] Doctors and mental health experts have also trained officials of the National Disaster Response Force and the State Disaster Response Force, launching a 24 × 7 mental health helpline that caters to all districts of J&K [122]. Driven by a recognition of the impact of violence on mental health, Help Foundation has provided counseling in the border areas of the Kupwara district and set up the first mental health counseling center in Kashmir. [Stakeholder F8, virtual interview, August 2021.] These indicate that the problems of capacity and awareness surrounding the question of mental health are being tackled. [Stakeholder C2, virtual interview, July 2021.]

A number of private schools have come up across J&K in recent years. According to 2016 data, 2,787 out of a total 14,352 primary, middle, and high/higher secondary schools in the state were privately owned, accounting for around 60,000 of 140,000 students [123]. [Stakeholder D3, virtual interview, July 2021.] Border communities have exhibited an interest in opportunities beyond government as is the case with communities in the rest of the state. However, in border areas, even the army must contend with the issues of staffing and disruption due to violence as other schools do, which reflects in the establishment of few Goodwill Schools in remote areas. [Stakeholder F5, virtual interview, March 2021; Stakeholder D2, virtual interview, June 2021.] On the other hand, few in these villages have the financial wherewithal to send their children to private boarding schools away from border areas. [Stakeholder D6, virtual interview, July 2021; Stakeholder D2, virtual interview, June 2021.] In some cases, civil society groups have helped establish mohalla schools. [Stakeholder E4, virtual interview, February 2021.] Needless to say, while this works as a temporary measure, such arrangements lack both the necessary infrastructure and the formal approval of the authorities for them to replace proper educational institutions.

Finally, constant uncertainty and the threat of violence have prevented employment generation by private players. For example, those in the region's apple and walnut industries have advocated for investments in technology, training, and facilities [124]. However, the constant threat of violence has so far disincentivized those from outside the region from investing their time, effort, or capital in these industries.

REFERENCES

1. 2013. Border Tension Affecting J&K: Omar. Business Standard, November 14. https://www.business-standard.com/article/pti-stories/border-tension-affecting-j-k-omar-113111400676_1.html.
2. For data for 2014–16, see Ceasefire Violations by Pakistan. 2017. Press Information Bureau, Government of India. https://pib.gov.in/newsite/PrintRelease.aspx?relid=168802. Accessed 11 January 2023; for data for 2017, see Unstarred Question No. 2981. 2018. Lok Sabha, Government of India. https://loksabha.nic.in/Questions/QResult15.aspx?qref=10557&lsno=16. Accessed 11 January 2023; for data for 2018–20, see Unstarred Question No. 149. 2021. Lok Sabha, Government of India. https://loksabha.nic.in/Questions/QResult15.aspx?qref=10557&lsno=16. Accessed 11 January 2023.

3. 2019. 15 Animals Killed, Houses Damaged in Pak Shelling. The Tribune, September 22. https://www.tribuneindia.com/news/archive/j-k/15-animals-killed-houses-damaged-in-pak-shelling-836228.
4. "Army Neutralises Unexploded Pakistani Shells near Kashmiri Homes [VIDEO]," *Times Now News*, June 23, 2020. https://www.timesnownews.com/india/article/Army-neutralises-unexploded-pakistani-shells-near-kashmiri-homes-video/610839. Accessed 11 January 202.
5. For data for 2014–2016, see Ceasefire Violations by Pakistan. 2017. Press Information Bureau, Government of India. https://pib.gov.in/newsite/PrintRelease.aspx?relid=168802. Accessed 11 January 2023; for data for 2017, see "Unstarred Question No. 2981"; for data for 2018–20, see "Unstarred Question No. 149."
6. "SDG India Index."
7. Verma, Mohinder. 2017. No Toilets, Drinking Water for Students but Govt Claims Turnaround in Education Sector. Daily Excelsior, January 10. https://www.dailyexcelsior.com/no-toilets-drinking-water-for-students-but-govt-claims-turnaround-in-education-sector/.
8. "SDG India Index," 96.
9. Bhat, Bisma. 2020. Poor Show in Class X Exam: Nine Govt Schools Record Zero Percent Result. Kashmir Monitor, January 11. https://www.thekashmirmonitor.net/poor-show-in-class-x-examnine-govt-schools-record-zero-percent-result/.
10. Union Territory and District Factsheets, Jammu & Kashmir, National Family Health Survey (NFHS)-5. 2020. International Institute for Population Sciences and Indian Cultural Forum. http://rchiips.org/nfhs/NFHS-5_FCTS/COMPENDIUM/Jammu_Kashmir.pdf. Accessed 1 June 2023.
11. 2020. Cross-Border Shelling a Constant with Exam Preparation for Students. The Tribune, October 20. https://www.tribuneindia.com/news/schools/cross-border-shelling-a-constant-with-exam-preparation-for-students-158577.
12. Economic Survey 2017. Directorate of Economics and Statistics, Planning Development & Monitoring Department, Government of Jammu and Kashmir. 224. https://ecostatjk.nic.in/pdf/publications/ecosurvey/2017.pdf. Accessed 11 January 2023.
13. Unstarred Question No. 2108. 2021. Parliament of India, Lok Sabha, House of the People, Government of India. https://loksabha.nic.in/Questions/QResult15.aspx?qref=26363&lsno=17. Accessed 11 January 2023.
14. Digest of Statistics 2019–20. 2021. Directorate of Economics and Statistics, Finance Department, Government of Jammu & Kashmir. https://ecostatjk.nic.in/pdf/publications/digeststat/2019-20.pdf. Accessed 1 June 2023.

54   D. PAL ET AL.

15. 2017. Poonch: Pakistan's Mindless Shelling Scars Education in Schools of Jammu and Kashmir. India Today, July 22. https://www.indiatoday.in/fyi/story/jammu-kashmir-poonch-pakistan-shelling-ceasefire-violation-schools-1025779-2017-07-22.
16. Pargal, Sanjeev. 2017. Pak Army Trains Guns on Kids, 261 Rescued; Schools Closed on LoC. Daily Excelsior, July 19. https://www.dailyexcelsior.com/pak-army-trains-guns-on-kids-261-rescued-schools-closed-on-loc/.
17. ANI (@ANI), Twitter post, February 27, 2018. https://twitter.com/ANI/status/968381412117278721. Accessed 11 January 2023.
18. Pargal, Sanjeev. 2017. Jawan, Child Killed; 3 Injured in Heavy Pak Shelling on LoC. Daily Excelsior, July 18. https://www.dailyexcelsior.com/jawan-child-killed-3-injured-heavy-pak-shelling-loc/.
19. Yasir, Sameer. 2018. Education First Casualty in India-Pakistan Cross-Border Firing along LoC: Residents Forced to Dump Kids' Future and Flee to Save Lives. Firstpost, January 24. https://www.firstpost.com/india/education-first-casualty-in-india-pakistan-cross-border-firing-along-loc-residents-forced-to-dump-kids-future-and-flee-to-save-lives-4317523.html.
20. Economic Survey 2008–09. Directorate of Economics and Statistics, Planning and Development Department, Government of Jammu and Kashmir. 7. https://ecostatjk.nic.in/pdf/publications/ecosurvey/2008-09.pdf. Accessed 11 January 2023; 2022. J-K: Unemployment Rate of 46 pc in Stark Contrast to Govt Claims, Says NC. ThePrint, March 20. https://theprint.in/india/j-k-unemployment-rate-of-46-pc-in-stark-contrast-to-govt-claims-says-nc/881192/; Unemployment Rate in India. Centre for Monitoring Indian Economy. Last modified 10 January 2023. https://unemploymentinindia.cmie.com/. Accessed 11 January 2023.
21. Economic Survey 2014–15: Volume-I. 2015. Directorate of Economics and Statistics, Planning and Development Department, Government of Jammu and Kashmir. 11. https://ecostatjk.nic.in/pdf/publications/ecosurvey/2014-15.pdf. Accessed 11 January 2023.
22. Wani, Fayaz. 2022. 'Hami Asto': Border Tourism Gains Momentum in Jammu and Kashmir. New Indian Express, September 29. https://www.newindianexpress.com/nation/2022/sep/29/hami-asto-border-tourism-gains-momentum-in-jammu-and-kashmir-2503080.html; Malik, Shafat. 2022. Ceasefire Brings Hope, Puts Gurez on Tourism Map. Rising Kashmir, December 27 http://risingkashmir.com/ceasefire-brings-hope-puts-gurez-on-tourism-map.
23. "Economic Survey 2014–15: Volume-I," 126.

24. Digest of Statistics 2020–21. 2021. Directorate of Economics and Statistics, Finance Department, Government of Jammu & Kashmir. https://ecostatjk.nic.in/pdf/publications/digeststat/2020-21.pdf. Accessed 1 June 2023.
25. "Economic Survey 2008–09," 6.
26. Economic Survey 2013–14. 2014. Directorate of Economics & Statistics, Government of Jammu and Kashmir. 6. http://14.139.60.153/bitstream/123456789/5353/1/Economic%20Survey%20J%26K.%202013-14.pdf. Accessed 11 January 2023.
27. "Digest of Statistics 2019–20."
28. Economic Survey 2009–10. 2010. Directorate of Economics & Statistics, Planning and Development Department, Government of Jammu and Kashmir. 1, 3. https://ecostatjk.nic.in/pdf/publications/ecosurvey/2009-10.pdf. Accessed 11 January 2023.
29. Ali, Nawal and Fouziya Tehzeeb. 2021. A Ghost That Haunts': Living with Landmines in Kashmir. Al Jazeera, January 27. https://www.aljazeera.com/features/2021/1/27/a-ghost-that-haunts-living-with-landmines-in-kashmir.
30. 2009. Need to Address the Problems Faced by People in Udhampur Parliamentary Constituency, Due to Fencing near International Border. Fifteenth series, vol. 3, Second session of Lok Sabha, Government of India. https://eparlib.nic.in/bitstream/123456789/758357/1/2007_II.pdf. Accessed 13 June 2023.
31. Hussain, Afaq, and Nikita Singla. 2020. Peace-Through-Trade At the Line of Control. Bureau of Research on Industry and Economic Fundamentals. https://www.briefindia.com/wp-content/uploads/2020/10/Peace-through-trade-at-the-Line-of-Control_BRIEF.pdf. Accessed January 11 2023.
32. Sharma, Arjun. 2022. 3 Years on, J&K Bizmen Want Cross-LoC Trade Resumed. The Tribune, March 2. https://www.tribuneindia.com/news/j-k/3-years-on-jk-bizmen-want-cross-loc-trade-resumed-374329.
33. Sengupta, Dipanker, Ershad Mahmud, and Zafar Iqbal Choudhary. 2012. Cross-Line of Control Trade: Peacebuilding and Economic Potential. Conciliation Resources. https://rc-services-assets.s3.eu-west-1.amazonaws.com/s3fs-public/IPK_LoC_trade_peacebuilding_web.pdf. Accessed 1 June 2023; For 2008–09, figures for import from Pakistan through the trade facilitation center (TFC) at Salamabad, Uri are unavailable. For 2012–13, Salamabad's TFC's data ends at January 2013, while for Chakkan-da-Bagh's TFC in Poonch, it ends at November 2012.
34. Zarfar, Safwat. 2019. 'Our Lives and Property Are at Stake': As Cross-LoC Trade Halts, Kashmiri Traders Lament Losses. Scroll, May 4. https://scroll.in/article/921849/our-lives-and-property-are-at-stake-as-cross-loc-trade-halts-kashmiri-traders-lament-losses.

35. Joshua, Anita. 2013. We Have No Intention of Escalating Tensions: Pakistan. The Hindu, January 11. https://www.thehindu.com/todays-paper/tp-national/we-have-no-intention-of-escalating-tensions-pakistan/article4296723.ece.
36. 2013. Ceasefire Violation: Indo-Pak Trade Affected at LoC. Zee News, March 4. https://zeenews.india.com/news/nation/ceasefire-violation-india-pak-trade-affected-at-loc_832940.html.
37. Kumar, Vinay. Pakistan Agrees to Attend Flag Meeting in Poonch Today. The Hindu, January 13. https://www.thehindu.com/todays-paper/Pakistan-agrees-to-attend-flag-meeting-in-Poonch-today/article12303518.ece.
38. Bhat, Rayees Mohammad and B. Rangaiah. 2015. Exposure to Armed Conflict and Prevalence of Posttraumatic Stress Symptoms Among Young Adults in Kashmir, India. *Journal of Aggression, Maltreatment & Trauma* 24:740–52. https://doi.org/10.1080/10926771.2015.1062449.
39. Bhat and Rangaiah, "Exposure to Armed Conflict," 740–52; Dar, Aehsan Ahmad. 2021. The Relationship of Risk and Protective Factors with Mental Health among the Youth in Kashmir. *International Journal of Behavioral Sciences* 15:201–06. https://doi.org/10.30491/ijbs.2021.275631.1492.
40. 2011. Oral Presentations and Specific Topics. *European Journal of Psychotraumatology* 2:62–126. https://doi.org/10.3402/ejpt.v2i0.7234.
41. Hoffman and Duschinski, "Contestations Over Law," 501–30.
42. "Muntazar Kashmir Mental Health Survey Report 2015."
43. "Oral Presentations," 62–126.
44. "Economic Survey 2014–15: Volume-I," 11.
45. Lateef, Adil. 2016. Solar Power Plant Worth Lakhs Lying Defunct at SDH Uri. Daily Excelsior, May 23. https://epaper.dailyexcelsior.com/2016/5/23/?id=49261.
46. Farooqi, Owais. 2021. Bandipora Hospital Finally Gets a Blood Bank. Greater Kashmir, November 21. https://www.greaterkashmir.com/kashmir/bandipora-hospital-finally-gets-a-blood-bank.
47. "Economic Survey 2009–10."
48. Rural Health Statistics 2021–22. 2022. Statistics Division, Ministry of Health and Family Welfare, Government of India. https://main.mohfw.gov.in/sites/default/files/RHS%202021-22_2.pdf. Accessed 1 June 2023.
49. Sudhan, Garima. 2021. In Poonch, Broken Healthcare System Has Left People to Suffer. Kashmir Walla, October 28 https://thekashmirwalla.com/in-poonch-broken-healthcare-system-has-left-people-to-suffer/.
50. Rural Health Statistics 2020–21. 2021. Statistics Division, Ministry of Health and Family Welfare, Government of India. 93–108. https://main.mohfw.gov.in/sites/default/files/rhs20-21_2.pdf. Accessed 12 January 2023.
51. Districts of Jammu and Kashmir. Population Census 2011. https://www.census2011.co.in/census/state/districtlist/jammu+and+kashmir.html. Accessed 12 January 2023.

52. Saroha, Sakshi. 2018. 25 Government Teachers Suspended in Jammu & Kashmir's Rajouri District. Jagran Josh, September 27. https://www. jagranjosh.com/news/25-government-teachers-suspended-in-jammu-kas hmirs-rajouri-district-147027.
53. Brara, Sarita. 2013. Fault Lines at the Frontlines. The Hindu, September 27. https://www.thehindu.com/todays-paper/tp-in-school/fault-lines-at-the-frontlines/article5172499.ece.
54. 2016. Net Services to Be Suspended Today. Daily Excelsior, June 21. https://epaper.dailyexcelsior.com/2016/6/21/; 2019. Schools in Jammu and Kashmir within 5 Km of International Border and LoC to Be Closed Today, Exams Rescheduled. Firstpost, February 28. https://www.firstpost. com/india/schools-in-jammu-and-kashmir-within-5-km-of-international-border-and-loc-to-be-closed-today-exams-rescheduled-6167611.html.
55. Tele-Medicine, Sher-I-Kashmir Institute of Medical Sciences, Soura, Srinagar. https://www.skims.ac.in/index.php?option=com_content&view=article&id=119:tele-medicine&catid=37:supportive-services&Itemid=114. Accessed 12 January 2023; 2022. Jammu & Kashmir: Centre Launches First Free Telemedicine Service in Kathua. Mint, February 13. https://www.livemint.com/news/india/jammu-kashmir-centre-launches-first-free-telemedicine-service-in-kathua-11644722895778.html.
56. Peerzada, Aamir. 2021. Education Interrupted: Kashmir Students Climb Mountain to Cross Digital Divide. BBC News, June 23. https://www.bbc.com/news/av/world-asia-57568521.
57. Snowber, Syed. 2021. 16.7% Students Drop out from Schools at Secondary Level in J&K. Morning Kashmir, December 22. https://morningkashmir.com/kashmir/16-7-students-drop-out-from-schools-at-secondary-level-in-jk/.
58. Rehman, Saleem Ur, Asif Jeelani, and SM Salim Khan. 2022. Analysis of Maternal Mortality in Jammu and Kashmir: A Retrospective Study Based on Review of Field Data. *Asian Journal of Medical Sciences* 13:56–61. https://doi.org/10.3126/ajms.v13i4.41351.
59. 2016. Patients Suffer as Lone MRI Machine of GMCH Goes Out of Order. Daily Excelsior, July 6. https://epaper.dailyexcelsior.com/2016/07/06/?id=51173; Shukla, Ajai. 2018. Five Civilians Killed, Two Injured on LoC as Pakistan Ups the Ante. Business Standard, March 19. https://www.business-standard.com/article/current-affairs/five-civilians-killed-two-injured-on-loc-as-pakistan-ups-the-ante-118031800527_1.html.
60. Puri, Luv. 2004. Border Villages Caught between Two Fences. The Hindu, July 29. https://www.thehindu.com/todays-paper/tp-national/tp-new delhi/border-villages-caught-between-two-fences/article27646487.ece.
61. Bhat, Bisma. 2019. Kashmir's Schools, Colleges Double up as Bunkers for Military; Students Forced to Depend on Tuitions, Notes in Absence

of Classes. Firstpost, November 30. https://www.firstpost.com/india/kashmirs-schools-colleges-double-up-as-bunkers-for-military-students-forced-to-depend-on-tuitions-notes-in-absence-of-classes-7720351.html.
62. Akmali, Mukeet. 2012. Poor Infra Keeps JK From DCT. Greater Kashmir, December 30. https://jammu-kashmir.com/archives/archives2012/kashmir20121230c.html.
63. "SDG India Index," 128.
64. "Digest of Statistics 2019–20."
65. Unstarred Question No. 5973. 2018. Parliament of India, Lok Sabha, House of the People, Government of India. https://loksabha.nic.in/Questions/QResult15.aspx?qref=67841&lsno=16. Accessed 11 January 2023.
66. Parliamentary Debates: Official Report, 30 July, 2014. 2014. Report No. 16, Rajya Sabha Secretariat, 124–25. https://cms.rajyasabha.nic.in/UploadedFiles/Debates/OfficialDebatesDatewise/Floor/232/F30.07.2014.pdf. Accessed 12 January 2023.
67. Ibid.
68. Parliamentary Debates: Official Report, 07 September, 2011. 2011. Report No. 25, Rajya Sabha Secretariat, 136–50. https://cms.rajyasabha.nic.in/UploadedFiles/Debates/OfficialDebatesDatewise/Floor/223/F07.09.2011.pdf. Accessed 12 January 2023.
69. Unstarred Question No. 588. 2018. Parliament of India, Lok Sabha, House of the People, Government of India. https://loksabha.nic.in/Questions/QResult15.aspx?qref=62056&lsno=16. Accessed 12 January 2023.
70. Majid, Zulfikar. 2021. 8,500 Underground Bunkers Constructed along Jammu Border. Deccan Herald, December 27. https://www.deccanherald.com/national/north-and-central/8500-underground-bunkers-constructed-along-jammu-border-1065104.html.
71. Ibid.
72. 2021. Bunkers for Border Dwellers. Daily Excelsior, December 29. https://www.dailyexcelsior.com/bunkers-for-border-dwellers/.
73. N. Das, Krishna and Mukesh Gupta. 2019. India Builds Bunkers to Protect Families along Pakistan Border. Reuters, February 27. https://www.reuters.com/article/us-india-kashmir-border-idUSKCN1QG20Y.
74. Bhasin Jamwal, Anuradha, and Shuchismita. 2012. Women's Voices from Jammu and Kashmir. *Journal of Borderlands Studies* 27:95–104. https://doi.org/10.1080/08865655.2012.687533.
75. Ibid.
76. Unstarred Question No. 2285. 2015. Parliament of India, Lok Sabha, House of the People, Government of India. https://loksabha.nic.in/Questions/QResult15.aspx?qref=26424&lsno=16. Accessed 12 January 2023.

77. 2013. Over 600 People Shifted Due to Border Shelling. Indian Express, October 29. http://archive.indianexpress.com/news/over-600-people-shifted-due-to-border-shelling/1188687/.

78. Annual Action Plan for the Year 2019–20 Under Border Under Border Area Development Programme (Health & Medical Education Department). Planning Development & Monitoring Department, Government of Jammu and Kashmir. http://jkplanning.gov.in/pdf/1. H&ME.xls. Accessed 12 January 2023; Indian Public Health Standards (IPHS) Guidelines for Sub-Centres. 2012. Directorate General of Health Services, Ministry of Health & Family Welfare, Government of India. https://nhm.gov.in/images/pdf/guidelines/iphs/iphs-revised-guidlines-2012/sub-centers.pdf. Accessed 12 January 2023.

79. 2014. Div Com Inaugurates Revenue Counseling Cell, Launches Aapka School Aapka Gaon Scheme. Daily Excelsior, October 24. https://www.dailyexcelsior.com/div-com-inaugurates-revenue-counseling-cell-launches-aapka-school-aapka-gaon-scheme/.

80. District/Department-Wise Proposed Allocation from 2020–21 to 2023–24. Planning Development & Monitoring Department, Government of Jammu and Kashmir. https://jkplanning.gov.in/pdf/BADP-distt-deptt.pdf. Accessed 12 January 2023.

81. Unstarred Question No. 298. 2023. Parliament of India, Lok Sabha, House of the People, Government of India. https://loksabha.nic.in/Questions/QResult15.aspx?qref=24463&lsno=14. Accessed 12 January 2023.

82. District-Wise Proposed Action Plan under BADP for the Years 2020–21 to 2023–24. Planning Development & Monitoring Department, Government of Jammu and Kashmir. https://jkplanning.gov.in/pdf/BADP%202020-24.pdf. Accessed 12 January 2023.

83. 2022. Families of 5 Lakh Women to Get Golden Cards. Greater Kashmir, July 8. https://www.greaterkashmir.com/health/families-of-5-lakh-women-to-get-golden-cards.

84. Hameed, Fayaz. 2020. Kupwara's Border People Hail Lg's Helicopter Announcement. Kupwara Times, October 1. https://www.kupwaratimes.com/kupwaras-border-people-hail-lgs-helicopter-announcement/.

85. "Union Territory and District Factsheets."

86. 2021. Rs 20 Cr Project Approved for Mobile Medical Units, Veterinary Dispensaries in Tribal Areas. Kashmir Reader, August 28. https://kashmirreader.com/2021/08/28/rs-20-cr-project-approved-for-mobile-medical-units-veterinary-dispensaries-in-tribal-areas/.

87. Select List for the Posts of Medical Officers (Allopathic) in the Health & Family Welfare Department—Appointment/Postings of Medical Officers Thereof. Daily Excelsior. https://www.dailyexcelsior.com/wp-content/uploads/2021/01/10510-done.pdf. Accessed 12 January 2023;

Select List for the Posts of Medical Officers (Allopathic) in the Health & Family Welfare Department—Cancellation as well as Appointment/Postings of Medical Officers Thereof. Daily Excelsior, Excelsior House. https://www.dailyexcelsior.com/wp-content/uploads/2021/02/11761-done4.pdf. Accessed 12 January 2023.

88. National Mental Health Programme. Directorate of Health Services, Kashmir, Union Territory of Jammu and Kashmir. https://www.dhskashmir.org/nmhp.php. Accessed 12 January 2023; Bhat and Rangaiah, "Exposure to Armed Conflict," 740–52.

89. State Development Report: Jammu and Kashmir. Planning Commission, Government of India. http://14.139.60.153/bitstream/123456789/5331/1/State%20Development%20Report.%20Jammu%20%26%20Kashmir.pdf. Accessed 12 January 2023; Parliamentary Debates: Official Report, 07 May, 2010. 2010.Report No. 32, Rajya Sabha Secretariat. 149–51. https://cms.rajyasabha.nic.in/UploadedFiles/Debates/OfficialDebatesDatewise/Floor/219/F07.05.2010.pdf. Accessed 12 January 2023; Parliamentary Debates: Official Report, 01 December, 2016. 2016. Report No. 12, Rajya Sabha Secretariat. 119–20. https://cms.rajyasabha.nic.in/UploadedFiles/Debates/OfficialDebatesDatewise/Floor/241/F01.12.2016.pdf. Accessed 12 January 2023.

90. 2018. Jammu and Kashmir: Remedial Classes for Students of Border Areas to Overcome Academic Losses. DNA India, January 24. https://www.dnaindia.com/india/report-jammu-and-kashmir-remedial-classes-for-students-of-border-areas-to-overcome-academic-losses-2578082.

91. 2016. CM Launches School Management Information System. Daily Excelsior, December 30. https://www.dailyexcelsior.com/cm-launches-school-management-information-system-2/.

92. Economic Survey 2016. 2016. Directorate of Economics and Statistics, Planning Development & Monitoring Department, Government of Jammu and Kashmir. 53. https://ecostatjk.nic.in/pdf/publications/ecosurvey/2016.pdf. Accessed 11 January 2023.

93. Economic Survey 2017. 2017. Directorate of Economics and Statistics, Planning Development & Monitoring Department, Government of Jammu and Kashmir. 231.

94. 2013. Corruption, Favoritism Rule Education Department in J&K. Kashmir Pulse, February 15. https://kashmirpulse.com/featured/corruption-favoritism-rule-education-department-in-jk/4142.html.

95. Malik, Bismah. 2013. Govt Orders to Fill Regular Teaching Vacancies in 2 Yrs—Fill up 24,000 Vacant Posts in 6 Months on Merit Basis: Assn. The Tribune, May 8. https://www.tribuneindia.com/2013/20130509/kashmir.htm#5; 2018. Biased Approach Of Govt Towards Rehabar-E-Taleem-Teachers. Kashmir Observer, January

16. https://kashmirobserver.net/2018/01/16/biased-approach-of-govt-towards-rehabar-e-taleem-teachers/.

96. Masood, Bashaarat. 2012. A Long Wait for Temporary Teachers. Indian Express, October 7. https://indianexpress.com/article/news-archive/web/a-long-wait-for-temporary-teachers/.

97. 2016. Mid Day Meals Cooks in Balakote without Wages. Daily Excelsior, January 4. https://www.dailyexcelsior.com/mid-day-meals-cooks-in-balakote-without-wages/.

98. Brara, "Fault Lines at the Frontlines."

99. 2013. Govt Plans to Bring Ordinance on Right to Education. The Tribune, December 11. https://www.tribuneindia.com/2013/20131212/j&k.htm.

100. 2016. Priya Inspects Border Schools. Daily Excelsior, January 2. https://www.dailyexcelsior.com/priya-inspects-border-schools/.

101. Parliamentary Debates: Official Report, 01 December, 2016. 2016. Report No. 12, Rajya Sabha Secretariat. 119–20. https://cms.rajyasabha.nic.in/UploadedFiles/Debates/OfficialDebatesDatewise/Floor/241/F01.12.2016.pdf. Accessed 12 January 2023.

102. Secretary-General Laid a Copy of the President's Address to Both the Houses of Parliament Assembled Together on the 12th March, 2012. 2012. Parliament of India, Lok Sabha, House of the People, Government of India. https://loksabha.nic.in/Debates/Result15.aspx?dbsl=6342. Accessed 12 January 2023; 2013. J&K Youth Shun Job Project, Thanks to Poor Salaries & Placements. The Hindu, September 9. https://www.thehindu.com/todays-paper/tp-national/jk-youth-shun-job-project-thanks-to-poor-salaries-placements/article5162097.ece.

103. Umeed. Jammu & Kashmir Rural Livelihoods Mission. https://jkumeed.in/projects/umeed/. Accessed 12 January 2023.

104. Kishanganga Hydroelectric Power Project Displaces Dard Tribe and Local Villagers in Bandipora. Land Conflict Watch, Nut Graph. https://www.landconflictwatch.org/conflicts/kishanganga-hydroelectric-power-project. Accessed 12 January 2023.

105. Dutta, Soumik. 2019. Indian Army's Project Roshni Lights Up Remote Villages in J&K with Solar Lights. Mercom India, May 7. https://mercomindia.com/roshni-lights-up-remote-villages-jk-solar-lights/.

106. 2021. Pakistan Fires at Indian Soldiers. The Hindu, July 9. https://www.thehindu.com/todays-paper/pakistan-fires-at-indian-soldiers/article4896399.ece.

107. 2016. Medical-Cum-Veterinary Camp Organized. Daily Excelsior, March 22. https://epaper.dailyexcelsior.com/2016/03/22/?id=46630; 2016. Army Organized Eye Camp Cum Sadbhavana Mela. Daily Excelsior, August 24. https://epaper.dailyexcelsior.com/2016/08/24/?id=53041.

108. 2016. Army Conducts Medical-Cum-Veterinary Camp. Daily Excelsior, February 7. https://epaper.dailyexcelsior.com/2016/2/7/?id=44770; 2014. Army Holds Medical Camp. Daily Excelsior, June 18. https://epaper.dailyexcelsior.com/2014/6/18/?id=18799; 2014. Army Organizes Medical Camps. Daily Excelsior, October 31. https://epaper.dailyexcelsior.com/2014/10/31/?id=24727.
109. 2014. RR Organizes Free Medical Camp. Daily Excelsior, September 19. https://epaper.dailyexcelsior.com/2014/9/19/?id=23020.
110. 2013. Army Initiates Medical Training for Youth. Daily Excelsior, July 23. https://epaper.dailyexcelsior.com/2013/7/23/?id=4373.
111. Chinar Corps—Indian Army (@ChinarcorpsIA), Twitter post, May 5, 2021. https://mobile.twitter.com/ChinarcorpsIA/status/1391582855776460808. Accessed January 2023.
112. 2015. Operation Sadbhavana: 7800 Jammu and Kashmir Youths Went on Educational Trips in Three Years. Economic Times, December 21. https://economictimes.indiatimes.com/news/defence/operation-sadbhavana-7800-jammu-and-kashmir-youths-went-on-educational-trips-in-three-years/articleshow/50271238.cms.
113. "About Operation Sadbhavana."
114. Ibid.
115. 2016. Army, JKEDI Conduct Skill Development Programme. Daily Excelsior, April 22. https://www.dailyexcelsior.com/army-jkedi-conduct-skill-development-programme/; 2016. Army Organises Career Guidance Seminar. Daily Excelsior, May 19. https://www.dailyexcelsior.com/army-organises-career-guidance-seminar/.
116. 2015. Army Organizes IT Course for Girl Students. Daily Excelsior, December 21. https://www.dailyexcelsior.com/army-organizes-it-course-for-girl-students/; 2016. Army Starts Basic Computer Course for Students. Daily Excelsior, February 6. https://www.dailyexcelsior.com/army-starts-basic-computer-course-for-students/.
117. Suri, Anirudh. 2004. NGOs in Kashmir: Agents of Peace and Development? Report No. 2, *Institute of Peace and Conflict Studies*. https://www.files.ethz.ch/isn/29038/2_NGOs_in_Kashmir.pdf.
118. Ibid.
119. 2016. Free Medical Camp Organized. Daily Excelsior, February 1. https://epaper.dailyexcelsior.com/2016/02/01/?id=44523; "Five kilometers from the border" has been estimated through Google Earth.
120. 2016. Guv Urged to Rehabilitate Persons Rendered Disabled in Shelling. Daily Excelsior, February 14._ https://epaper.dailyexcelsior.com/2016/02/14/?id=45053.
121. Aqeel Hussain, Sayed. Mental Health GAP Training in Kashmir in Collaboration with Royal College of Psychiatry and DHServices

Kashmir Supported by WHO. https://sayedaqeel.wixsite.com/kndri/home. Accessed 12 January 2023.

122. Ibid.; 2021. COVID-19: J-K Launches Round-The-Clock Mental Health Helpline 'Sukoon'. Mint, July 1. https://www.livemint.com/news/india/covid19-j-k-launches-round-the-clock-mental-health-helpline-sukoon-11625104886838.html.

123. Economic Survey 2016. 2016. Directorate of Economics and Statistics, Planning Development & Monitoring Department, Government of Jammu and Kashmir. 10–11. https://ecostatjk.nic.in/pdf/publications/ecosurvey/2016.pdf. Accessed 11 January 2023.

124. Amin, Imran Ul and Anisa Jan. 2017. Financing the Apple Industry of Jammu and Kashmir: A Review of Literature. *IOSR Journal of Business and Management* 19:17–22. https://www.researchgate.net/publication/316056880_Financing_the_Apple_Industry_of_Jammu_and_Kashmir_A_Review_of_Literature; Amin Malik, Irfan. 2021. Why Kashmir's Walnut Industry Is on the Back Foot. Moneycontrol, September 18. https://www.moneycontrol.com/news/trends/features/why-kashmirs-walnut-industry-is-on-the-back-foot-7474791.html.

CHAPTER 6

Conclusion

Abstract This chapter summarises the study, explores the effect of recent trends such as the peace brought on by the reaffirmation of the 2003 ceasefire, and examines the way forward for the topic under study.

Keywords Jammu · Kashmir · Development projects · Infrastructure · State capacity · Indian Army · Cross-border violence

The February 2021 reaffirmation of an eighteen-year-old ceasefire agreement between India and Pakistan has led to easing restrictions along the border, allowing development projects to gather speed. This includes work on roadways, water supply, telecommunications, and health infrastructure along with conversations about coordination between different agencies working in the region [1]. As the Indian minister for tourism informed the parliament in July 2022, over 10 million tourists visited J&K for the first time ever in the first six months of the year [2]. Local and central governments are tapping into tourism in offbeat areas of border districts such as Kupwara, Baramulla, Poonch, and Rajouri [3]. [Stakeholder D11, virtual interview, August 2021.] While these developments point to improving conditions, there is an inherent understanding among the locals that the peace, in the absence of structural issues being

© The Author(s), under exclusive license to Springer Nature Switzerland AG 2025

D. Pal et al., *Violence and Development Along the India-Pakistan Border in Jammu & Kashmir,*
https://doi.org/10.1007/978-3-031-84927-5_6

addressed, is temporary at best. This is evident in the fact that in over eighteen months without CFVs, permanent security structures along the border have not been dismantled.

This study finds that the impact of years of cross-border violence has fundamentally altered how border communities live, trapped in a cycle of confinement, displacement, and migration. Each of these is directly or indirectly a result of an increase in escalation along the IB and the LoC. CFVs lead to the closure of schools and health centers and prevent agricultural workers and traders from attending to their work through curfews and shutdowns, including telecommunication shutdowns. Periodic disruptions have impacted education, employment, and medical processes. As a result, illnesses have been left untreated, students consistently miss school days, and new economic ventures have failed to take root.

Beyond the first-order impact, CFVs continue to affect lives even when the borders are peaceful. Coincident factors, such as the response of the state to violence, conditions such as terrain and climate, and the sociopolitical environment critically influence the lives of villagers. The constant threat of violence discourages skilled resources, such as teachers and doctors, from serving in these areas. On the ground, agricultural land is used for security infrastructure such as access roads and watchtowers. Over time, unable to deal with the breakdown of social and communal fabric, residents of these villages migrate to safer areas, often with little certainty about economic, educational, or other prospects. Policies such as building bunkers to protect locals during CFVs offer temporary relief but cannot act as substitutes for long-term development.

An important result of the violence and the presence of security agencies is a proliferation of military infrastructure and a tightening of security measures. This reflects in more stringent verification processes, restrictions on the movement of non-security personnel, and curbs on access to public infrastructure. Coupled with these measures, the ubiquity of violence in everyday life has led to the security agencies assuming a central position in the day-to-day fabric of the region at the cost of the civilian administration. The administration's role has also diminished due to the expanding role of the army beyond a security provider as a development and service provider. Despite this, the threat of violence against local populations has continued, as can be seen in the number of village council office-bearers stepping down. By 2012, personal threats against them had forced as many as eighty *panches* and *sarpanches* across the region to resign from their posts [4].

The model of military-led development has unsettled the balance of institution-led development in the border areas. The core competency of security forces is not in carrying out tasks that are ideally suited for a village council or a district administration. Additionally, in line with the mandate of the military, the development work carried out by security forces is aimed at contributing to a "hearts and minds" strategy and not necessarily ensuring effective delivery of public goods. As a result, growth in these areas is often in spurts, based on the availability of resources and the preference of military commanders instead of a well-designed plan. While the presence of security personnel creates some jobs, infrastructure, and avenues for service delivery, they hinder growth because of restricted movement, curfew mandates, stop-and-search operations, and shutdowns.

This study uses primary source data to offer a detailed bottom-up perspective on the relationship between CFVs and everyday life on and along the border. It suffers from the absence of organized data specifically on villages close to the LoC and the IB. Demographics, population density, and the availability of resources along the border in these districts differ from conditions in parts of the district further inland. The instability arising from the interaction of violence with factors such as terrain and the sociopolitical conditions have also not been observed in detail. This has remained unrecorded as even large-scale studies such as the National Family Health Survey consider districts as the unit for sampling exercises. As a next step, studies examining the issue of SDGs in border communities would benefit from detailed data collection that considers not just violence as a catalyst but also the aforementioned associated factors.

REFERENCES

1. Majeed, Tahir. 2022. Developing the Border Areas of J&K. Greater Kashmir, November 30. https://www.greaterkashmir.com/todays-paper/editorial-page/developing-the-border-areas-of-jk.
2. Unstarred Question No. 35. 2022. Parliament of India, Lok Sabha, Government of India. https://loksabha.nic.in/Questions/QResult15.aspx?qref=38982&lsno=17. Accessed 12 January 2023.
3. Majid, Zulfikar. Ceasefire Dividends: Govt Plans to Start Border Tourism in Kashmir. Deccan Herald, February 2. https://www.deccanherald.com/national/north-and-central/ceasefire-dividends-govt-plans-to-start-border-tourism-in-kashmir-1077312.html.

4. Parliamentary Debates: Official Report, 13 December, 2012. 2012. Report No. 15, Rajya Sabha Secretariat. 123–24. https://cms.rajyasabha.nic.in/UploadedFiles/Debates/OfficialDebatesDatewise/Floor/227/F13.12.2012.pdf. Accessed 12 January 2023.

Printed in the United States
by Baker & Taylor Publisher Services